Quotes and Testimonials

"A great book. I enjoyed reading it and learnt a lot. Unlike other business books, I read every page as I didn't want to miss anything. There is a lot we at PruHealth can learn from this."
Shaun Matisonn, CEO, PruHealth

"Well presented and very readable. The concepts and frameworks used are relevant and helpful and I particularly like the way Dr Greenfield builds them up into a diagnostic framework at the end of the book."
Prof Colin Carnall, Associate Dean of Executive Programmes, Warwick Business School

"There are excellent examples throughout – historic, modern, aspirational and realistic. The language is very user-friendly and I love the tools and techniques."
Sharon Collier, Head of People Development, Somerfield

"A terrific book and everything it says resonates with my experience – there is nothing with which I disagree. I love the difficulty and adaptability questionnaires."
Humphrey Claxton, former MD of BNFL Engineering Ltd

"Many management books are either too esoteric or treat the reader as an idiot! However, this book is highly readable and extremely practical – what I liked most was learning from the successes and failures of other organisations."
Tony Thwaites, Chairman, Eveden Group

"This book contains a potent mix of hard experience, academic research and penetrating analysis – it provides the key to unlocking organisational change."
Peter Smith, Chairman of South Yorkshire Probationary Area

"A great reference for any leader who wants to liberate people's capacity to transform organisational performance."
Mark Ashton, Managing Partner, Resolve

"This book has a real practical edge as well as well as shedding new light on the why people so often struggle with change."
Andrew Stevens, Head of Talent and Leadership Development, Northern Trust Bank

"An essential reference and guide for any manager embarking on change. I will ensure that every manager in my organisation has a copy and that they can demonstrat⋯ ⋯es of Change."
N⋯ ⋯s Plc

D1076722

For a complete list of Management Books 2000 titles
visit our website on http://www.mb2000.com

THE 5 FORCES OF CHANGE

A blueprint for leading successful change

Anthony Greenfield

2000

The cartoon on page 74 is reproduced by kind permission of P. C. Vey.

The photograph on page 82 is reproduced by kind permission of Ross Party Agency Ltd.

First published in 2008 by Management Books 2000 Ltd
Forge House, Limes Road
Kemble, Cirencester
Gloucestershire, GL7 6AD, UK
Tel: 0044 (0) 1285 771441
Fax: 0044 (0) 1285 771055
Email: info@mb2000.com
Web: www.mb2000.com

British Library Cataloguing in Publication Data is available

ISBN 9781852526054

Printed and Bound by Digital Book Print Ltd

For Abigail

Acknowledgements

I would like to thank the following people for reviewing my book and helping to give it its final shape; Abigail Levin, Peter Smith, Sharon Collier, Humphrey Claxton, Shaun Matisonn, Gill Jeffries, Colin Carnall, Mary Fairas, Andrew Stevens and Susan Glicher.

About the Author

Anthony Greenfield has experienced the ups and downs of large-scale organisational change first-hand through his work with leading organisations in the UK, US and South Africa. He is also a keen observer of the many changes taking place all around us, from the drive to improve children's eating habits to major corporate mergers. He has spent many years developing his understanding of what makes some organisations and some leaders successful at bringing about change whilst others fail, culminating in the 5 Forces of Change (www.5forcesofchange.com). Anthony continues to work closely with organisations that want to achieve lasting improvement in their performance. He also runs seminars, workshops and training courses on successful leadership of change as well as publishing numerous articles on the subject. Anthony is a Partner at Resolve (www.rgr.uk.com) and a Director of Abigail Levin Consultancy Ltd.

Contents

Chapter 1

Introduction: People and Change

"It is not the strongest of the species that survives, nor the most intelligent that survives. It is the one that is the most adaptable to change."

Charles Darwin [1809 – 1882]

1.1 The trouble with change

Major organisational change should be avoided at all cost. It sucks up time, energy and emotion, distracts you from your main purpose, disrupts operations, annoys your people, undermines morale and rarely delivers the promised benefits. The statistics make grim reading. 70% of change programmes fail[1], 75% of all re-engineering projects fail to achieve their aims[2] and 83% of all mergers and acquisitions fail to increase shareholder value[3].

Looked at another way, the world of work is shifting at such a mind-boggling rate that we have little choice but to continually change or risk being left behind. Information Technology continues to shrink the world and revolutionise the way organisations operate. Between the years 1750 and 1900, the world's entire scientific knowledge doubled. Now it doubles every 1-2 years. In January 2008, there were 875 million internet shoppers worldwide[4]; in 1993 there were none. Success is no longer a matter of being the fittest or the smartest. It is about being the most adaptable to change. Any enterprise that can introduce new ideas and new approaches frequently and effortlessly has a huge advantage. It is the role of a modern leader to make this possible.

Whereas organisations may have little choice but to change, *people* do have a choice, and for organisations to change successfully it is essential that they find a way to carry their people with them. Large-scale change requires people to invest a great deal of energy and emotion in getting to grips with new methods and in living with extended periods of uncertainty. The role of a leader is to guide, support and sustain people through the trials and tribulations of change. Better still, it is to engage the enthusiasm and ingenuity of people in bringing about swift, painless and sustained change.

At the heart of the matter is the way we experience and respond to change. Extended periods of uncertainty, associated with any major change, cause us stress and anxiety. We are reluctant to let go of familiar things and to abandon tried and trusted approaches in favour of novel and unproven ideas. We like to feel in control of our destiny and hate to look foolish when struggling to do something new for the first time. We want to know where we are going and how we are going to get there, and when the ground begins to shift under our feet we lose confidence and find it hard to remain effective.

On the flip-side, we are capable of amazing things. We love to rise to a challenge and derive enormous satisfaction from overcoming obstacles and succeeding against the odds. We are innately curious creatures who enjoy exploring new avenues, coming up with better ways of doing things and learning new skills. So our response to a given change can vary dramatically depending on how we experience it and how we are led through it.

The key to success, and the subject of this book, is to work *with* the grain of human nature rather than against it. Like a master of martial arts, you must turn opposing forces to your advantage instead of meeting them head on. In short, if you can help people to become more certain, more in control, more connected, more purposeful, more confident and more successful during change then they will achieve extraordinary results.

This book allows you to learn from the successes and failures of others. It equips you with the understanding and tools you need to become one of those rare leaders who is able to bring about lasting organisational change with a minimum of fuss.

1.2 Heroes of change

Change may be problematic but there is evidence of it all around us. The last hundred years has been unprecedented in the history of mankind in terms of the change that we humans have brought about. So what can we learn from people and organisations that have been successful in bringing about change? Who are the "heroes of change" and what have they understood about human nature that can help us achieve our goals?

One of the best-known heroes of change is Mohandas "Mahatma" Ghandi who led the movement for independence for India from the British Empire through non-violent protest in the 1940s. One of the most powerful things Ghandi did was simply to embody the change he wanted to bring about. For instance, he dispensed with Western dress in favour of a traditional white cotton robe signalling his championing of ordinary people and an India built proudly on Indian traditions not Western values. One brief story illustrates his style of leadership. A mother visited Ghandi with her daughter and asked him to persuade her daughter to give up her habit of eating sugar as it was damaging her teeth and making her overweight. The Mahatma told the mother and daughter to go away and return the following week. On their return, he asked the girl to give up eating sugar. Her mother, somewhat put out, asked why they had had to wait a week for him to do as she had requested. "That's because a week ago I too ate sugar" was his reply. As he once famously declared, "We must become the change we want to see."

The TV chef Jamie Oliver has, in his own way, become a hero of change. He made big news in the UK by working with schools, and eventually the British government, to introduce healthier lunches into schools in the face of rising childhood obesity. As part of his BBC television series, entitled "Jamie's School Dinners", he stepped into one school and worked with the head 'dinner lady' to prove that children could be persuaded to eat more fruit and vegetables and to give up fried chicken nuggets and chips. Once he had proved that it could be done in one school, he trained dozens of dinner ladies from other schools in the art of creating healthy meals on a tight budget that would appeal to children. One great technique Jamie used to overcome the reservations of a particular group of children who steadfastly refused to even try the healthy food was to get them into the kitchen and to teach them how to prepare healthy meals for themselves. By giving them a better understanding of food and a sense of ownership and control over the creation of healthy dishes they became converts to the cause of healthy eating. The important lessons we can learn from Jamie's successes and failures are covered in Chapter 3.

Any parent who has helped a nervous child dispense with bicycle stabilisers and begin learning to ride their bicycle unaided is a hero of change. They know that any girl or boy approaching something they find daunting needs plenty of encouragement. Even the slightest improvement or momentary unaided pedalling needs to be praised to the skies to help them persevere when facing the perils of grazed knees and damaged pride. Without support through the initial wobbles the shiny new bike, bought at great expense, will simply gather dust in the garage. Self-belief is just as important for adults when trying out new things. People should be recognised for having a go at applying new working methods even if initial results are poor. They need encouragement and support if they are going to persevere through the initial wobbles and win through in the end.

Another unlikely hero of change was the person who tens of thousands of years ago first came up with the notion of a ceremony – I am assuming here that the first ceremony was (as most early ceremonies were) a ritual celebration of change, be it a marriage, a death, the passing of a season, or a coming of age. The idea of celebrating change in this way showed an early understanding of the way that humans need to recognise and deal with certain kinds of change, particularly the kinds of change which involve a passage to a new life and a new set of relationships. This understanding can also help us today, in our quest for transformational change in the workplace.

On a different note, Martin Luther King, the great American civil rights activist in the 1950s and 1960s, dared people to dream of a day when people of different races and religions could live side by side in harmony. In his famous 1963 speech, "I Have a Dream", delivered to a crowd of thousands on the steps of the Lincoln Memorial in Washington D.C., he painted a vivid and compelling image of a brighter, more egalitarian future. Here is an excerpt:

> I say to you today, my friends, that in spite of the difficulties and frustrations of the moment, I still have a dream. It is a dream deeply rooted in the American dream.
>
> I have a dream that one day this nation will rise up and live out the true meaning of its creed: "We hold these truths to be self-evident; that all men are created equal."
>
> I have a dream that one day on the red hills of Georgia the sons of former slaves and the sons of former slave-owners will be able to sit down together at the table of brotherhood.
>
> I have a dream that one day even the state of Mississippi, a desert state sweltering with the heat of injustice and oppression, will be transformed into an oasis of freedom and justice.

I have a dream that my four little children will one day live in a nation where they will not be judged by the colour of their skin but by the content of their character...

King knew that if people could glimpse, even for one moment, this brighter, more equal future then it would help them share his faith and conviction despite the hardships and opposition they faced at that time. He also linked the past (quoting from the American Declaration of Independence) to the present and to the future, an important technique for framing change as evolution, not revolution. For your part, you may not be changing the political landscape of a powerful nation, but without strong conviction and the ability to communicate a brighter vision of the future you cannot expect people to follow you along what may be a difficult and uncertain path.

Another more prosaic but important hero of change is the first person who tore gaping holes in their jeans and then stuck them back together with safety pins. In the cycle of change, this type of hero is the 'Innovator', the trendsetter who dares to be different and to take the lead. Others who followed the trend, the so-called Early Adopters, began to spread the idea until what had once been thought outlandish became mainstream and fashionable – and a glamorous model (Liz Hurley) was famously photographed wearing a £10,000 Versace dress held together with safety pins at a London film première (*Four Weddings and a Funeral*).

The fashion industry is a vast machine that manages to drive a perpetual cycle of innovation and change. It takes a trendsetter to set the direction and the fashion gurus to bring it to the mass audience. To bring about change in your organisation you need to allow the trendsetters to take the lead and the Early Adopters to spread the message.

So what can we learn from these disparate heroes? What do they know that will help us bring about successful change? The answer is that in their different ways they have managed to address some basic human needs that must be satisfied for change to take root. What these needs are and how they can be fulfilled is revealed in the pages of this book.

1.3   The myth of "resistance to change"

For thousands of years human beings existed primarily as farmers, happy to plough fields and raise animals (still a way of life for millions around the world). The pace of life was dictated by the regular progression of the seasons; there was a time for planting and a time for harvesting. Society was held together by traditions and unchanging beliefs. Everyone knew their place and what was expected of them. The rate of change was gentle and one tradition slowly gave way to the next over generations.

The human race would have been wiped out long ago if people accepted every strange new idea without a thought. We like to work things through in our minds, test them out and gradually absorb them into our way of life. Times of major upheaval, such as the Industrial Revolution, have brought with them great hardship and misery for many as familiar ties are broken and only slowly replaced by a new order.

Even positive change comes at a price. We all know that exciting and desirable changes can feel as stressful as undesirable ones. Think of examples in your own life, like starting a better job or moving to a new home. You may have been fed up with your old job but at least you could operate comfortably within it, and your new home might have more space for the kids but you cannot help feeling nostalgic about the old place despite it being cramped.

We all have a conservative streak. It may be larger or smaller according to our nature, our experience and our age. Some people are naturally mistrusting of new ideas and lots of people become more set in their ways as the years pass. On the other hand, many older people in the West are now finding a new lease of life and making dramatic changes in their 60s and beyond, choosing, for example, to do voluntary work in distant and inhospitable corners of the globe. People can and do make remarkable changes when the conditions are right.

Compared to mankind's early history the speed of change in modern times is astonishing. The world of our children is almost unrecognisable to our parents. Technology, mobile communications and the internet have shrunk the world and transformed our lives. A consequence of this revolution is that frequent change has become part and parcel of working life and, if anything, the pace of change is accelerating. All of this comes at a price in human terms. Sudden or dramatic change can be a source of great emotional turmoil as we are forced to live with a high degree of uncertainty and relinquish tried and trusted methods for unfamiliar ones. However, organisations that want to survive and prosper in the long term have little choice but to continually re-adjust or re-invent themselves to keep pace with changes in the environment. At the same time, they cannot risk alienating their people or leaving them behind altogether in the rush to stay ahead of the game.

Much has been written about overcoming people's "resistance to change", but in reality people rarely set out to oppose change through sheer bloody-mindedness. It is, however, all too easy to provoke them into it, especially when they have experienced badly managed change in the past. At the root of the problem is not people's inability to adapt and work positively to bring about change, but the way that change is so often handled by organisations. *That is why this book is about removing the underlying motives for resistance to change rather than dealing with resistance to change itself.*

Stirring up opposition to change is very easy. You could, for instance, suddenly announce to people who have worked in the same role for many years that their job is going to change dramatically overnight and that they will be working with new people using new methods under a new payment structure. For good measure, you might add that their job title will change from "Manager" to "Co-ordinator". You can probably imagine the consequences. They certainly would "resist" change. More likely they would be extremely annoyed. People don't react badly to change; they do react badly to poor leadership. This example may seem extreme and something you would never contemplate doing, but most experienced people will have come across circumstances at work where change has been handled at least as badly if not worse. For example, I recently came across a case of a senior director in a major organisation being fired by text message! Moreover, there are myriad other more or less subtle ways to really infuriate people when introducing a new initiative.

The good news is that by anticipating and responding to people's basic needs during change not only can you avoid triggering negative reactions, but you can also harness their talent and energy to help you deliver a far more successful change than you might ever have imagined.

So how is it done? First off, you need to appreciate what makes people tick – the basic things that drive them to do things like strive for promotion, work hard to meet a deadline or help others succeed. Next, you need to understand how these basic drivers are affected when something comes along that shakes up the status quo and threatens to knock things off balance. Then you must learn how to meet people's needs during periods of transition and so reap the benefits of working with a team that is pulling with you rather than against you. This book leads you through each of these stages.

Change has many potential pitfalls, but if you help your people to adapt, your chances of success will be vastly increased.

1.4 Root causes

In business and the public sector, continuously re-thinking and reshaping the way we do things has become part of everyday working life. The need to constantly manage transition is not just a matter for specialists like project managers or consultants but is now recognised as a core management skill. Leaders know that organisations that cannot adapt efficiently will wither and die.

Most modern organisations invest huge quantities of time, money and emotional energy each year in planning, organising and executing change. Despite all this, managers and executives frequently find themselves in the aftermath of a major initiative wondering what has actually been achieved. Too often the answer is 'not very much'. Worse than that, their people become progressively more sceptical about improving things and the next big initiative has even less chance of delivering the goods.

There are countless examples of organisations that have spent a fortune on new warehouses, business re-organisations, marketing campaigns, acquisitions, IT systems, training programmes, incentive schemes and all manner of new initiatives that have seen little or no return on their investment. One common cry is that people's performance has not improved – "If only they would exploit the new systems and new ways of working to their full potential we would be producing better products at half the cost." So why are things not improving? Has all the investment been misplaced?

The answer is that change can and does succeed, and the small minority of organisations that are able, time and again, to truly exploit change have a significant competitive edge. It is not for nothing that piles of books have been written on the subject and that an industry dedicated to the management of change has sprung up over the last two decades.

Yet with all this, little has been done to dig beneath the surface issues of change and understand the underlying root causes. Much has been written, for instance, about the need for strong leadership and good communication during times of change – and the need to draw people towards a compelling vision of the future, and get people to take ownership of change. This is all sound advice, but any approach needs to be appropriate to the situation and applied in the right way at the right time. What is needed is the recipe for success not just a list of possible ingredients.

If, for instance, you wanted to build a bridge, it would seem like a good idea to hire some earthmovers and a crane and to equip yourself with steel girders and a large quantity of concrete. Using a bit of common sense and an enormous amount of sweat, not to mention lost sleep, you might even build some sort of a half decent bridge by following a "wing and a prayer" approach.

Many of us, however, would prefer to begin by studying the terrain that the bridge was due to be built on and to understand its purpose before we embarked on such a major undertaking. We would wonder how much weight the bridge might need to support, if there was a river to be spanned or even whether a simple rope bridge would suffice. Before drawing up any plans, those of us who are not already qualified civil engineers would want to understand how steel and concrete can be brought together successfully, elegantly and economically to create our bridge. We would want to appreciate the interplay between the materials and the stresses and strains that it would have to withstand to allow heavy traffic to pass over it safely.

Many leaders and managers follow the "wing and a prayer" approach when they come to deal with change. Often, they will know about the basic building blocks for successful change, such as good communication, through experience or from what they have learnt from others. They pull all this understanding together using common sense, gut feel and a good deal of blood, sweat and tears. What they lack is a clear appreciation of why these building blocks are so important and how they interplay. As a result, it is very difficult to apply the right technique in the right way according to the needs of the situation. Furthermore, if things go awry, as they almost certainly will at some point, there is a great temptation for leaders to stop applying these methods altogether if they don't understand how and why they work.

Wholesale change means learning to operate in new ways and dealing with unfamiliar issues. But there is much more to it than the inconvenience of having to readjust your approach. When organisations and people encounter change, some fundamental forces of human nature come into play provoking strong emotional responses ranging from fear and anxiety through to disorientation, immobilisation and anger.

By understanding the nature of these forces and how to work with them you can use the materials at your disposal to build a bridge that suits the terrain in which you find yourself and meets the purposes of the transition you wish to achieve. Ignore them and they will almost certainly derail your plans. That is why great leaders are students of human nature and develop a strong sense of how to influence and inspire people, especially when they want to lead them into uncharted territory.

This book provides you with a practical guide to harnessing the forces that motivate people to help you succeed with your next change initiative.

1.5 The 5 Forces of Change

Through the work of Maslow[4] and Herzberg[5] we have come to understand what motivates people at work. Herzberg identified 'hygiene' factors, such as pay, that serve to *de-motivate* people when they are absent, and *motivating* factors, such as achievement, that serve to motivate people to strive hard at work. It is these motivating factors that help us understand why it is that people respond to change in the way that they do.

By examining how motivating factors are affected by different types of change in a range of different types of organisation, I have identified five key areas of motivation that are strongly affected by organisational change. These human drivers, illustrated in Figure 1.1 and summarized below, which I have named the 5 Forces of Change, form the basis of this book. The next five chapters are dedicated to examining each one in turn and uncovering the practicalities of addressing them successfully during organisational change.

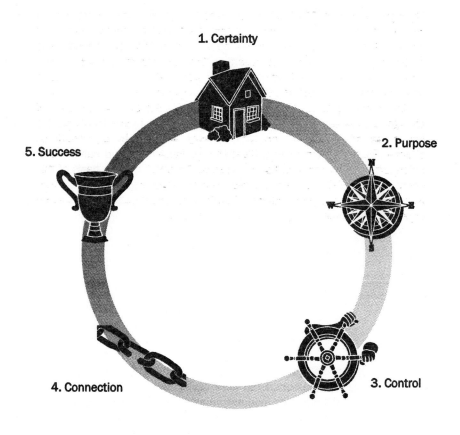

Figure 1.1 The 5 Forces of Change

1. Certainty

An immediate consequence of impending change is uncertainty. At worst, people fear for their jobs - at the very least, they can become unclear about what the future holds and their role within it. This causes anxiety and leads to distraction from work and a drop in performance. Chapter 2 is about creating certainty in uncertain times.

2. Purpose

During periods of stability it is relatively easy to appreciate the purpose of what you are doing. Whether you are building cars or teaching children it is not hard to understand the overall objective. As an organisation changes course things can become foggy. People's sense of direction is diminished and they become less confident about what they are doing. Chapter 3 deals with the need for leaders to provide a clear sense of purpose and to communicate it with conviction.

3. Control

Organisational change, especially when it is imposed from the outside, can lead to strong feelings of unease as people sense that they have lost control over their working lives and become victims to outside forces. This can cause people to rebel against change or to quietly opt out of it. Giving people greater control over their destiny is the subject of Chapter 4.

4. Connection

We all form strong attachments to people and things. We identify ourselves with the job we do and the way we do it. We value our relationships with colleagues, customers and suppliers. We become attached to our organisation, our team, or even our desk. When things change we need to change or break these connections and form new ones. Chapter 5 looks at how help people end old connections and adopt new ones with a minimum of heartache.

5. Success

Anyone who has tried out new techniques when playing sport or following a change at work knows that performance often gets worse before it gets better and that there is a strong temptation to revert back to tried and trusted methods rather than persevere with new ones. Chapter 6 deals with the importance of failure during change and the need to nurture success to create the momentum necessary to ensure change takes root.

1.6 About this book

If you are a leader (a manager or executive of any sort) who knows what it is like to grapple with the challenges of bringing about successful change or if you are about to embark on an important change of any description for the first time, then this book is for you. It draws on many people's experiences of managing large-scale projects, including my own, as well as the insight of management experts. Above all, it is a practical aid to anyone who wants to know how to improve his or her leadership of change.

This book is about how *people* become involved with change, how they take it on board and how they make the most of it. How you go about designing new processes, new organisation structures, new information systems or how you define your organisation's culture or even how you plan an office move is entirely up to you. This book focuses on helping you introduce and instil change by working with and through your people no matter what the nature of the change might be.

Sudden or dramatic change does not sit comfortably with human nature and much of this book is about the clash between people's fundamental motives and the consequences of change. Understanding this is the starting point for appreciating the difficulties of change and how to overcome them. This book uncovers the human needs underlying the way we respond to change.

Section 1 of this book, comprising Chapters 2-5, deals with each of the Five Force of Change in turn, illustrating them through real examples of successes and failures, and explaining how best to work with them to achieve your goals.

Then **Section 2**, comprising Chapters 7-10, deals with the practicalities of applying the 5 Forces of Change to successfully implement organisational change.

In Chapter 7, we examine a paradox of change; on the one hand we are curious creatures who enjoy new things, but at the same time we place great store in the predictable. We also examine how our desire for variety can be used to tip the balance in favour of change.

Chapters 8 and 9 deal with the realities of introducing major changes that affect people in a range of ways, both good and bad. They provide tools and techniques that can be used to help people implement change successfully whilst minimising any downturn in performance and ensuring that any change introduced results in lasting improvement.

Chapter 10 brings together many of the important themes of this book to describe the characteristics of great change leadership.

This book contains many examples from work and society at large to illustrate how other people have dealt with change in the past. Through these stories you will begin to understand what you need to do to steer your own teams through the difficult waters of change. You will also see that the root of the problem invariably lies not with the proposed new processes, new technology or new structures but with the way they are taken up by people. You will discover the deep-rooted human needs that govern the way people respond to new ideas and the prospect of change. Great leaders seem to know instinctively how to tap into these needs to win people over, whilst others trip over them, often ending up worse off than before they started.

SECTION 1

The 5 Forces of Change

Chapter 2

Certainty

"A leader is a dealer in hope"

Napoleon Bonaparte

2.1 Mental maps

If you have ever been travelling to an important meeting and waited on a station platform for a delayed train, you know the meaning of uncertainty. As time ticks by, you may consider the possibility of dashing to the car park and taking your chances on the motorway. As you glance at your watch for the fifteenth time you might begin mentally writing a petulant letter to the managing director of the train company calling his or her competence into question. Then, out of the blue, comes an announcement that your train has left the previous station and will be with you in 11 minutes, leaving you plenty of time to reach your meeting. As you board the train, thoughts of incompetent railway management evaporate and you begin contemplating a cup of coffee and the pre-reading for the meeting. Certainty has been restored.

These sorts of irritation are part-and-parcel of the stress and strain of modern working life. They cause short bursts of frustration that generally pass quickly. More serious problems arise when people experience high levels of uncertainty over long periods of time, as is often the case with major organisational change.

We all need a degree of certainty. At different times in our lives and for different people the level of certainty required may vary but, whoever we are, we all need people and things we can rely on. They can take on a variety of forms such as friends and family, a place to call home, a regular routine, a job or a dependable set of rules and beliefs to help us navigate our way through difficulties. They provide a firm foundation on which to base our lives, steady us in times of uncertainty and help make us feel safe and secure. Take them away and we are soon in trouble.

As every skilled interrogator knows, the first step to breaking down a person's resistance is to strip them of familiar things. Take away someone's possessions, isolate them from friends and family and even deprive them of the assurance that night follows day (by keeping them in constant light) and they become confused, distressed and more susceptible to questioning.

At work, we come to rely on things such as standard practices, organisation structures, business processes, values and cultural norms. Over the years, we create a **mental map** of how things work, how to get things done and how to deal with problems. We use this mental map to navigate through work, to guide our decisions and in our dealings with other people.

If we move to a new organisation, we spend many weeks trying to work out the unwritten rules about how people work together, acceptable and unacceptable behaviour, power relationships and the ethos of the organisation. Most of this is gathered through observation of our new colleagues; how do they talk to each other? How do they deal with crises? Do they show up to meetings on time? Consciously or unconsciously we gradually identify patterns of behaviour and cultural norms and pretty soon we conform to them and 'go native'. If we cannot adapt to our new surrounding it is likely that we will find work difficult. We may become isolated, unhappy and eventually leave. So a good mental map is vital to our success.

But when change comes along, certainty is the first casualty. Our mental map can no longer be relied upon to guide us. We need to make adjustments and test our new map against new experiences. For small changes, like an amendment to a procedure or the introduction of a new person into our team, we can make the adjustment with little apparent effort. For major changes, we may go through a great deal of turmoil as we are forced to make wholesale revisions to our mental map of the workplace. Following a change in organisational structure, for instance, new teams are formed and new roles created. As a result, people need to adjust to new ways of working together, new responsibilities and even new attitudes. This is most challenging in situations where people have done the same thing in the same way for many years, creating a mental map that is deeply ingrained and has become the indisputable truth.

Small changes may raise people's levels of stress for a while, but major changes can be a culture shock as mental maps are torn apart, causing severe disorientation. People can experience the sort of emotional roller-coaster ride more normally associated with extreme personal upheaval such as divorce or the loss of a loved one. There may be periods of denial, frustration and dejection before people eventually come to terms with the new reality. Without an effective approach that enables people to adjust to change they can easily become demoralised or even immobilised as they feel the rug being pulled from under them. The resultant drop in performance at work represents a serious danger to their organisation.

This chapter explains how uncertainty can be minimised during change, greatly increasing your chances of improving performance quickly and with a minimum of disruption to operations. In particular, we look at the importance of open and honest communication, a subject which may already be familiar to readers with extensive experience of change. We also highlight the importance of a clear vision of the future and the need for confident and determined leadership. Most importantly, in this chapter and in those that follow, we look at how leading change in the right way can motivate people to work with it rather than against it.

2.2   Crazy time

It is well known that the popular British comedian Eddie Izzard is a transvestite. During his live performances, his partiality for women's clothes and make-up doesn't seem particularly out of place as we are used to seeing performers in strange costumes on stage. However, he tells a number of great stories about how people react to him when he is going about his daily business wearing a dress. He recounts walking up to the counter in a corner shop and the shopkeeper staring at him obviously startled. The shopkeeper's brain registers 'a man in a dress' but is unable to process this information based on any past experiences and is reduced to mumbling idiotically. In the face of seemingly nonsensical information that does not fit into his mental map of the world, the shopkeeper is left stunned.

This is a great example of how people can react to a novel situation where past experience cannot be used as a guide to current behaviour. It gives us a strong clue as to one of the reasons why change is often stressful. Change requires us to abandon old approaches and to adopt a new and unfamiliar set of rules. It requires that we reprogramme our brains to be able to operate efficiently in a new environment. It involves a tricky process of adjusting to unfamiliar terrain requiring a period of trial and error characterised by uncertainty, apprehension and mistakes. No wonder then that people can become fearful or frustrated and respond in ways that obstruct change and damage organisational performance.

Negative reactions to major change can persist from when it is first announced until well beyond the time that the change has supposedly been installed and things should be back on an even keel. This difficult period of transition, often characterised by anxiety and confusion, is known to some people familiar with organisational change as 'Crazy Time'.

Take the example of a mass transport organisation that went from public to private ownership. Unsurprisingly, there was a good deal of uncertainty and concern amongst people at every level in an organisation that had a proud history of over 100 years of public service. What did private ownership entail? Would a new commercial focus mean longer hours or fewer jobs? Would shareholder's interests come above those of the travelling public?

As is typical of many large-scale organisational changes, the rumour mill went into overdrive and a lot of time and energy was diverted away from work to focus on people's personal worries. Some people expressed deep concerns and battled against changes while others tried to avoid it altogether in the hope that by keeping their heads down, the whole thing would blow over. But after a period of anxiety and frustration people learnt what was expected of them under the new regime and made a more or less successful transition.

However, in one corner of the organisation, the whole range of emotions and negative behaviours had yet to play out. This was the organisation's training centre, which was largely overlooked during the shift to private ownership. The focus of people's efforts during the transition period was on ensuring that operations continued to run smoothly and that investment in new infrastructure was driven forward. The training centre was left to its own devices.

Months later, problems became apparent. There were unreasonably long waiting times to get people onto basic training courses, including the Safety Training course, which was a prerequisite for almost all new recruits before they could start work. Even when people got on to courses, a large number of them were being failed by instructors. On top of that, operations managers were heavily critical of what people were being trained on and how they were being trained. A battle was developing between instructors who felt they were the guardians of high standards of practice and operations managers who felt that people were not being equipped for the practical commercial realities of the organisation. Some parts of the business were trying to set up their own training courses while others were trading insults with the training centre, including accusations of verbal and even physical abuse.

The training centre was still working with an old map of the world. This was immediately obvious on arrival at their premises where you were greeted by an old public service sign above the front door rather than the new company logo. On the one hand, instructors were in denial that things had changed, and on the other, they were battling against what they believed to be a drop in standards prompted by the advent of profit-driven privatisation.

The fact that the training centre was caught in a time warp was however not of their making. It was hard to blame them for not embracing change with open arms when they had not been given the wherewithal to do so. As a consequence, they inevitably clashed with the rest of the organisation and became a serious obstruction to successful change.

Any organisation going through major change has to face a difficult period of uncertainty as the old ways give way to the new ones (see Figure 2.1). The trick is to minimise the length and strength of Crazy Time by increasing people's level of certainty.

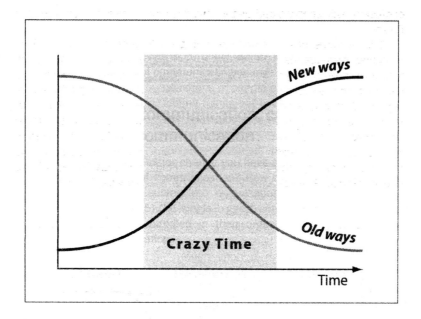

Figure 2.1 Crazy Time – the transition between new and old ways of working

2.3   Dip in performance

This book aims to help you reduce or eliminate the drop in performance that accompanies change. When people lack understanding about where they are heading and how they will cope when they get there, they become anxious about the future, confused about what is expected of them and frustrated by lack of clarity. As a result, they become distracted from the day job. Performance drops and customer service suffers. Uncertainty is one of the main causes of this loss of performance and so must be addressed proactively.

In the particular case of an organisation faced with being taken over or merged with another organisation, it is not unusual for some people to lose practically all of their motivation and drive. On the surface, they appear to continue to function as normal. However, in reality, they are simply going through the motions. Whilst people's mental maps are thrown into confusion they simply tread water until they get a clearer picture of the future.

It is at times of major change that great leaders come to the fore, providing reassurance and restoring confidence in the future. These leaders intervene early to establish certainty as quickly as possible so as to minimise the severity and duration of any disruption in performance. Figure 2.2 is a graphical illustration of the effect of great leadership in minimising the dip in performance associated with uncertainty (where performance can be measured in terms of sales, productivity, customer service, etc.). In the earlier example of the training centre in the privatised transport company, the absence of any discernible leadership of the change resulted in a spectacular drop in customer service.

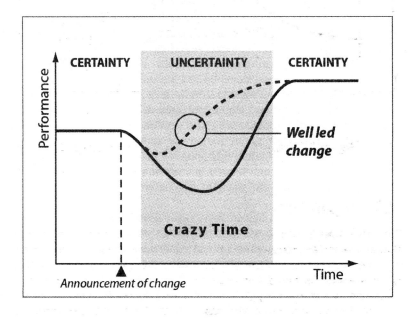

Figure 2.2 Minimising the dip in performance

2.4 Tolerance for change

Each of us responds differently to change according to the nature of the change, our circumstances and our personalities. Some of us may be 'change junkies', always looking for the latest trends and grabbing hold of novel ideas. Others may be naturally more cautious, waiting for things to be tried and tested before even contemplating change. In Chapter 7, we will see how most populations can be divided into distinct groups according to their propensity for change. Figure 2.3 illustrates a simple continuum where people on the right end favour 'Exploration' (i.e. new ideas and methods) and people on the left end favour 'Stability' (i.e. current ideas and methods).

Just for fun, you might want to test your own propensity for change by placing yourself in the continuum in response to five questions:

1. How willing are you to go and work abroad for a year starting in 2 months time? [An unreserved 'Yes' scores 10, 'maybe' scores 5 and 'definitely not' scores 0].

2. How involved are you in the latest trends on the Internet? (E.g. Do you buy and sell on the Internet? Do you have your own entry on My Space? Do you have your own blog?) ['Yes, I am into all the latest Internet trends' scores 10, 'some involvement' score 5 and 'I don't even know what they are' scores 0]

3. How happy would you be to move into an entirely new, more exciting role at work next week? [An unreserved 'Yes' scores 10 and 'Definitely not' scores 0].

4. How much is what you wear influenced by the latest fashion trends? ['Not at all' scores 0 and 'Completely influenced' scores 10]

5. Outside work, are you currently learning a major new skill or have you learnt one in the last 6 months? ['None at all' scores 0 and 'Several new skills' scores 10]

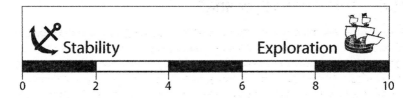

Figure 2.3 The Stability – Exploration Continuum

Change is in the eye of the beholder. Each of us will score ourselves according to our current circumstance, the nature of the change and our natural propensity for change. People with young children may want to work abroad but are likely to be concerned about the health and schooling of their children in foreign parts and so, most likely, will score themselves less than 10 on question one. We may have been dedicated followers of fashion at one time in our lives but now perhaps pay little or no attention to it.

People have different predispositions to change. Some are naturally cautious while others may learn caution from working in a risk-averse environment. Doing the same thing in the same way year after year will also make it far more challenging for people to change. When working on a major change project I am always relieved to find that at least some members of the senior team are relatively new to their roles. Such people are generally more likely to be willing to live through a period of uncertainty in pursuit of improved organisational performance as they are less emotionally attached to current ways of thinking and working. In Chapter 8, we will see how to measure people's tolerance for change so we can identify areas of concern and gauge how difficult the journey will be.

2.5 Leading people in uncertain times

It is in times of uncertainty when great leaders are worth their weight in gold. Great leaders have a strong vision of where they want an organisation to go which they communicate constantly and passionately. They help people imagine the future, let go of the past and ready themselves for change. They are a source of confidence and reassurance in difficult times and back their words up with actions. They are honest about the difficulties associated with change and foster trust – a vital ingredient of a successful change. A survey conducted in 2003 by the business research specialists Prosci[1], asked people within 288 different organisations about their experience of organisational change – the single greatest contributor to success identified by those surveyed was **executive sponsorship**. Effective sponsors "show visible and active support [for change], provide compelling justification for why the change is happening" and "communicate a clear understanding of the goals and objectives of change".

During periods of upheaval people look for clear and decisive leadership. In times of war, we are drawn to leaders who are courageous, confident and determined. During times of transformation, people will naturally take their cue from the demeanour, actions and words of their leaders. At a time when a leader might be feeling uncomfortable about their own future, they need to be a guide and a steadying influence. What they say in private must match what they say in public, and most importantly, their words must be backed up by their deeds. Nothing will kill a change quicker than half-hearted leadership. If a leader merely mouths the words or betrays their discomfort with the change then there is little chance that others will want to embrace it. Furthermore, leaders at every level need to be as one in communicating the change. They are all links in the same chain. It matters little to a soldier what the general says if the captain or the sergeant major say the opposite.

If you are leading a change you need to begin by working on yourself, eliminating your own doubts and redrawing your own map of the world. You need to leap into the river before encouraging others to take the plunge. You need to take it to heart and talk about it with conviction. As we saw in Chapter 1, Ghandi, the consummate leader, embodied the change he wanted to bring about and would not ask anyone to do anything he had not first done himself.

You must also help other leaders (especially those that report to you) to become self-assured about the change, reminding them that people will be more interested in their tone of voice, their confidence and their body language than in the words that they use. Even more than that, they will be convinced by their actions.

Some managers will feel like they are stuck in the middle between an enthusiastic leadership group promoting change and concerned employees wary of what it all means. It is at the middle management layer that change often breaks down. It is all too easy to assume that all managers will give their unquestioning support and get on with making the change happen. However, it is reasonable for them to have their own doubts about the change and unless they are brought on board (using the 5 Forces of Change) they can become a major blockage in the works. On top of this, they may be ill-equipped to manage their own teams through the change process and so either make a hash of it or avoid trying altogether. Gaining the confidence of mid-level leaders and educating them in the art of bringing about change are critical tasks for senior leaders. It is the mid-level leaders who are responsible for putting a vision of change into practice within their area of responsibility and for ensuring that the organisation continues to run smoothly during crazy time. If a large proportion of them they are not fully on board then change will not become a reality.

During times of change, when certainty is in short supply, effective leaders will do everything they can to ramp up levels of communication across their organisation. As with any difficult journey, people will want to know from the outset why they should leave the comfort and security of familiar surroundings. It is up to leaders to spell out the benefits of change and the dangers of staying put to help convince people that the trip will be worthwhile. They need to help people redraw their mental maps of the world as quickly as possible by erecting new landmarks and charting new terrain. Thus a vivid picture must be communicated of what it will be like at work once the change has taken place – how it will look, how it will feel, and what is expected of people in terms of tasks, roles, attitudes and behaviours. If people are to develop confidence that they will be able to travel safely to the new world they also need to know how they will be provided with the resources and support they need to succeed when they get there.

Effective communication is not about painting a rosy picture of change. It is vital that people are told the truth. In fact, being open about the difficulties that may lie ahead demonstrates your respect for people's intelligence and boosts people's confidence in you as a leader. When people are uncertain about what they can rely on, they need leaders they can trust. Furthermore, you should be up-front about uncertainty. Let people know that it is all part-and-parcel of the transition process and that it is alright to feel insecure. In this way, they can accept the feeling more easily, even joke about it and get on with the job in hand.

Trust is a particularly crucial issue when a change involves job losses. The people left behind inside the organisation may feel that the unwritten contract between the organisation and its employees has been broken and mistrust can easily take hold. Two important strategies that can help ensure that this does not happen are the fair and equitable treatment of those made redundant and a great deal of open communication. Choosing not to talk about difficult subjects for fear of stirring up bad feelings or having to handle difficult conversations will inevitably backfire as concerns are simply driven underground where they will fester.

In Chapters 3 and 4, we will see how a clear sense of purpose and a feeling of control over your work environment are essential ingredients of successful organisational change partly due to the fact that they boost people's levels of certainty. Before that, we will focus in more detail on the vital task of communicating change.

2.6 Communication, communication, communication

Think of a major change you have been involved in. What did people want in terms of communication? How did this compare to what they actually got? In a survey into organisational change conducted by Prosci (see Section 2.5) the single biggest complaint people had about how change had been handled in their organisation was ineffective or insufficient communication.

Take the example of how important changes were communicated in one financial services company. A common gripe amongst call centre sales staff was that the first time they got to hear about a new product or new promotional offer was when a customer asked them about it. Investigation into what had happened with a particular special offer revealed that the call centre staff had been informed about it several days in advance. However, the means of communication was a single sentence in a standard weekly update e-mail sent out to all staff covering a wide range of different issues. Only a small percentage of staff could recall reading that part of the email so in practice almost no communication had taken place.

In this age of the email, it is all too easy to assume that communication can be achieved at the click of a mouse. Communication is not a one-off event, especially where a large-scale change is involved. You may be a fabulous orator, but confidence in a major change cannot be conjured up out of thin air by a single presentation. We may fondly imagine that the polite applause at the end of a presentation signals the all clear for change, but it is just part of an extended process of winning people over. The measure of successful communication is not that it has been sent or received but that it has been acted on effectively.

Communication of change should be viewed as a process extending over time. People progress in stages from initial recognition of a change to understanding it, before moving on to testing it and accepting it. Finally, they absorb it fully into their lives and their mental maps of the world. People's needs vary according to the stage that they have reached in accepting change and so the style, content and means of communication must vary to match these needs. For instance, giving people a huge amount of detailed information the first time you talk to them about a major change is a waste of effort as all they really want is answers to the big questions about how they will be affected. Equally, using email to announce a major change to people whose roles are going to be heavily affected by it will undoubtedly lead to all sorts of misinterpretation in the absence of opportunities for dialogue. Not to mention the fact that people will feel insulted that you have not shown them the respect of speaking to them face-to-face on such a controversial issue.

The timing of communication is also crucial. Communicate too soon and you risk extending the period of uncertainty ahead of introducing a change. Communicate too late and you risk people feeling that you have been keeping it hidden and that they have not had sufficient opportunity to provide input or prepare for the change. Even when a change is going to be difficult and involve negative consequences for people, an open and inclusive approach is far more likely to achieve a positive outcome. Letting people work through the change for themselves helps them to feel more in control. They can come to terms with what's required far better than hiding the 'bad news' until the last minute and turning people into victims of change. See Chapter 4 for more on the subject of giving people control over change.

Figure 2.4 illustrates the gradual progression that people make from becoming aware of change to being fully committed to it. The dotted lines on the graph illustrate how support for change can fall away at any time along the way if the communication process stops or becomes ineffective putting the whole change back a step or derailing it altogether. People's support must never be taken for granted. Even after the change has supposedly taken place (e.g. new working practices have been launched) it is vital to keep up the dialogue as many people will still be weighing up the pros and cons of the change and can still easily backtrack or opt out.

Different people will progress at different speeds in becoming committed to a change. Some enthusiasts will have already established themselves in the new world while others are still cautiously testing the water. As we will see in Chapter 7, tipping the balance of opinion in favour of change requires the commitment of a large number people, including many who are wary of change, as well as the early adopters.

In the case of the privatised transport company referred to earlier, an entire division of the organisation (the training centre) was still stranded in the awareness stage whilst the rest of the organisation had long since settled into a new way of thinking and operating.

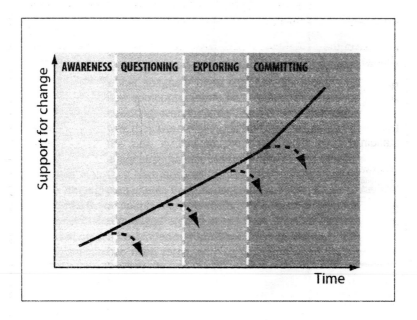

Figure 2.4 The Four Stages of Support for Change
(based on chart by Daryl Conner[2])

Each of the Four Stages of Support for Change (Awareness, Questioning, Exploring and Committing) illustrated in Figure 2.4, requires a distinct approach to communication. The Table in Figure 2.5 highlights key messages to be communicated during each stage.

Stage 1: Awareness	Stage 2: Questioning	Stage 3: Exploring	Stage 4: Committing
The causes of the change	Purpose for the change	Purpose of the change	Early successes
Purpose of the change	A multi-faceted picture of the future	New roles and structures	Recognition of those who are applying new practices
Benefits of change	Expectations of individuals following change	Detailed new skills, behaviours and attitudes	Progress against organisational improvement targets
Dangers of standing still	Answers to people's questions and concerns	Detail of the implementation plans	How to overcome teething problems
What will change		Details of training and post-implementation support	
Overall timing of change			
Major effects of change			
Opportunities for open dialogue			

Figure 2.5 Key information to communicate as support for change increases

Stage 1 - Awareness

In the Awareness Stage, people are exposed to the change for the first time. They have had little time to assess the likely impact of the change and to formulate detailed questions. Most likely, they just want answers to the most urgent questions, such as, "How will I and my colleagues be affected?" "Will I still have a job?" "Why do we need to change?" "When will it happen?" It is up to leaders to fill the information void. Do nothing and it will quickly be filled by misinformation and gossip leading to all sorts of unpredictable and largely negative consequences. People can become fearful and inward looking, less productive and less caring of customers.

The Awareness Stage is the time when you first set out a clear and compelling purpose for the change giving people a sense of direction and establishing a level of certainty (more on this in Chapter 3). It is time to paint a positive picture of the future where, for instance, current frustrations about access to data have been eliminated and to reinforce this with messages about the dangers of standing still, such as losing market share to a new more innovative competitor.

This is also the time to answer some of the basic questions about what, when, where, why and how. Importantly, this is your first opportunity to set the tone for how you plan to handle the change.

It is doubtful at this stage that you will have all the answers. It is possible that you will have very few. Be open about this. Explain that this is just the first step on a journey. Explain how you intend to get people involved, how they will have opportunities to ask questions and be kept informed along the way. Be open and honest also about the difficulties involved in making change happen. Recognise that you are asking them to invest their time and effort to make it work and that you need their support. Spend time answering people's questions. You need people's trust, so be clear about where you want to go and honest about not having all the answers.

Where possible, those who are most affected by the change (or at least a representative group of them) should be involved directly in formulating the plans so that they have a strong sense of ownership for the change (see Chapter 4). Whatever the case, people need to be taken on a mental journey and see the logic of the decisions that have led up to the change so that they can start to rationalise it and accept it.

It is all too easy when you are close to the detail of project to lose the ability to put yourself in the shoes of someone completely unfamiliar with what has been done. It is a rare expert who has the ability to explain their area of expertise clearly and succinctly to a complete novice. But this is what you need to do. So in setting out the vision for change you should explain the history of the initiative, how it came about and why each important decision has been made along the way. For instance, start by explaining how competitive pressures and market conditions mean that you need to adopt new technology to stay ahead of the game or risk losing sales and market share. Explain how you are going through a process of selecting the best new technology for the organisation and what this might mean for the people who are going to have to use it.

It also important not to fall into the trap of implying that people's efforts to date have somehow been misguided or faulty and need to be replaced by a superior new way of doing things. Belittling what has gone before can easily provoke people into defending the status quo (with which they strongly identify) and pick holes in the planned change. Rather, position the change as arising out of changed circumstances, such as new customer needs or new legislation. Make it clear how the approaches that have served you well in the past will no longer be as effective in the future.

Be aware of your audience in shaping your messages. Some people will welcome change and just want to get on with it, whilst others need evidence, logic and detail to convince them. Some are mainly concerned about how people will be affected and want assurances that the change has worked elsewhere. Others need to see a clear plan of action. Everyone is more or less interested in what it means for them and preferably how the change will benefit them in their daily lives.

There is a fine balance between providing people with information and making it clear that they have the opportunity to influence things. It is important, for instance, to show people a high level plan for the change to give them confidence that things are under control, but providing them with a detailed plan in which everything has already been decided denies them the opportunity to fill in the details for themselves, an opportunity which would promote a sense of ownership for the change, as is explained in Chapter 4.

Remember, this is just the first step in a long process of communication so don't expect too much at this stage. There will be some early enthusiasts who get it straight away and want it all to happen tomorrow but the majority will be slowly absorbing the messages and will need time to reflect before moving onto the next stage.

Stage 2 – Questioning

Once people have a general understanding of what is about to happen, they begin to formulate many more questions over the coming days and weeks. This is all part of them evaluating the change, getting to grips with how they will be affected and choosing how to respond to it. It is the crucial period during which you can eliminate doubts and win people over. It is important at this stage to go out of your way to encourage people to ask questions and voice concerns and to take time to respond to them (small group discussions, for instance, are useful in overcoming people's reticence to ask questions in large forums). Do not be afraid of awkward questions or people appearing to be negative. This is all just part of people testing things out and gives you better insight into their biggest concerns. The last thing you need is a hidden undercurrent of concern especially when merely exposing people to the facts can eliminate it. On top of that, welcoming difficult questions and responding to them honestly is an important means of setting the tone for change and fostering trust, a very important commodity during times of change.

Don't forget to reiterate the purpose and benefits of the change, something that cannot be repeated too often at each stage of the journey. Remember that communicating a message just once does not mean that it has been understood and absorbed.

Much effort is rightly spent in the time leading up to a change in explaining *what* is going to change, such as new team structures, new job roles and new working methods. What is often overlooked is an explanation of what it will be like to inhabit this new world. What will people be expected to achieve and how will they be expected to behave? What are the new rules and the new cultural norms? What will be rewarded and what will be unacceptable? Without answers to these questions, people can only develop a patchy mental map of the future, lacking detail and colour, and insufficient to enable them to navigate the new world effectively. During the Questioning stage and beyond, you need to communicate how it will feel to inhabit the future as well as describing it formally in terms of organisation structures, process and roles.

Too often, change fails to take root because people have not had future expectations spelt out to them. For instance, introducing a more entrepreneurial culture into an organisation where people are used to strong hierarchies and centralised control is doomed to failure if people are not told about the new rules of the game and what will now be expected of them. It is not enough just to tell people that they are empowered to make decisions for themselves and to innovate. They need, for instance, to understand and come to terms with the radically new role of their manager as a coach and facilitator rather than a boss.

It is also important to describe the structures, people, expectations, methods and traditions that will remain unaltered. This will reassure people that the future will not be too different from the past and helps ensure that in their haste to transform people do not cast off things that remain crucial to your organisation. Introducing a more entrepreneurial culture that encourages people to innovate, for instance, is not a licence to ignore the basic values of respect for colleagues or quality standards that have brought you success up till this point. Big changes provide an excellent excuse, if one is needed, for re-emphasising your organisation's unchanging ethos and values.

Stage 3 – Exploring

As the time for change approaches, detail becomes the order of the day as many people start preparing themselves to succeed in a changed environment. During this Exploration Stage, people will also begin to ask more about how the transition is going to be managed. They will be keen to know when and how they will be trained in new skills and how they will be supported during the difficult early stages of a change (when they may struggle to cope and be tempted to fall back on old ways of doing things), so now is the time to set out your proposed programme of training and ongoing support. Questions about your approach to implementing the change should be welcomed as an indication that people have started to prepare mentally for the journey. It also represents an ideal opportunity to engage people by involving them in determining how to implement the change in their part of the organisation.

People like to hear about change from their peers. There is nothing more powerful than the testimony of colleagues who have already made a successful transition to build confidence and understanding amongst those who have yet to experience it. People generally trust that their colleagues will share the same concerns as them, talk the same language as them and will be honest about the pitfalls as well as the benefits of making the change. So if you plan to introduce change in one part of your organisation ahead of the rest, bring some of the people who are involved in the first wave of change into the project team. They can then spread the word about how to make the change a success, and even work alongside their colleagues to implement the change in other areas of the organisation.

Much of the communication in the Exploration Stage takes place through some form of training. Having your team gathered together in a classroom or workshop represents a golden opportunity to set the standards and expectations for how people should operate in the new world as well as ensuring that they have the skills and knowledge to succeed. However, in the rush to meet project deadlines, training can be seen as a necessary evil. There may be much debate within the management team about the difficulties of taking people away from their day jobs and the expense of training venues. Many major projects trip up at the last hurdle due to poor training.

Take the example of a UK Government Agency that had managed its information on spreadsheets for many years. Over time, these spreadsheets steadily grew in number, complex and size until they eventually become hugely inefficient and nearly impossible to manage. So a decision was taken to install a new computer system that could do everything that the spreadsheets did only far more quickly and efficiently, saving enormous amounts of time spent entering data on multiple spreadsheets and trying to keep the whole spaghetti mess together. Six months later, when the shiny new computer system was up and running people were still double checking everything on the old spreadsheets. When asked about why they were doing this one user explained that they didn't trust the new system to get things right and anyway it didn't do everything that the old spreadsheets did. Asked about what training they had received on the new system they replied vaguely some consultants from the systems supplier did come in to train them for a couple of days before the system went live. One user then rummaged around in her desk drawers and eventually produced a thick binder entitled 'User Training Manual'. It turned out that there had been some teething problems when the system first went live, leading to people's doubts about its effectiveness. Closer inspection of the User Training Manual also revealed that the new system did everything the old spreadsheets did and more. Training had simply not been taken seriously, nor had it been backed up with support after implementation so a huge amount of time and effort was wasted in working with two systems in parallel.

This example may seem like an obvious case of poor management of change, but it is not simply an isolated incident. Even when people are equipped with the skills they need to be successful in their changed roles, things can still fall apart. If training focuses on developing people's skills and overlooks the need to instil a new understanding of how the organisation will operate following change and the new ethos required to make it successful (e.g. a greater focus on customers or on quality) then people will still fail to meet expectations.

Training and developing skills, attitudes and behaviours is an enormous subject in itself, but some of the key factors to consider when training people ahead of a change are:

- Visible support from executives for training (e.g. through personal endorsement).
- Use training to reinforce the purpose of the change.
- Set clear expectations for how people will work in the transformed organisation in terms of attitudes as well as activities.
- Dedicate the majority of the time spent in training to practising skills and behaviours through exercises and case studies.
- Ensure training is timed so that people get to apply what they have learnt as soon as possible.

Finally, there is great benefit to be had from getting line managers involved in delivering training. Not only does it illustrate their commitment to the change which will have a strong influence on their teams' readiness to accept it, but is also cements the change in the minds of the management team and ensures they have the wherewithal to coach their people effectively following the change.

Stage 4 – Committing

It is tempting at this, the Committing Stage, when the change has been put in place (e.g. new working processes have been launched), to assume that the change has 'happened' and everything can now return to normal. However, there will be a large swathe of people who will only now be starting to become convinced of the change in the face of hard evidence that it is up and running and delivering results.

Once a change has been set in place, the role of communication is to help ensure that the change is cemented into place. This involves broadcasting how the change is progressing, providing information on how to overcome the 'teething problems' which inevitably accompany any new initiative and, above all, keeping people bought into the process despite any drop in performance. Trumpeting early successes is vital for keeping up morale during this difficult transition stage and helping to ensure that people follow through to completion. It is up to the leaders to coach, encourage and support their teams and to act as role models for the new ways of working. Without all of this activity it is possible support for change will fall away at the final hurdle and all that has gone before will have been a waste of time.

Finally, it is sobering to recall how a certain proportion of the population respond to the prospect of massive, imminent and inevitable change. Take, for instance, the way some people react to the news of an approaching flood. Despite repeated warnings of danger to life and limb and clear evacuation procedures, there are always those who steadfastly refuse to abandon their homes until they are perched on the roofs of their houses with the water lapping around their ankles. There is a lot more to change than just loss of certainty as we will see in the chapters that follow.

Summary

Change causes uncertainty, which can lead to anxiety, confusion and a drop in performance levels. It is the job of an organisation's leaders to minimise any loss of performance by leading from the front and articulating a clear and compelling vision of the future.

Leaders should:

1. Build up their own confidence in the change before leading others and help other leaders do the same.

2. Lead from the front by being a confident role model for new attitudes and behaviours.

3. Educate senior leaders and middle managers in the art of leading successful change.

4. Build trust through open and honest two-way communication. Make it ok for people to express their concerns so that they can be dealt with out in the open.

5. View communication as a process, varying the style, content and medium according to people's needs and the stage of the journey.

6. Communicate the benefits of change and the danger of the status quo.

7. Help people to redraw their mental maps of the world by painting a vivid and multi-faceted picture of the future, including new expectations of people.

8. Where possible, involve people who have already transitioned to the new world to help persuade others to join them.

9. Provide people with thorough and practical training on the skills, attitudes and behaviours that they need to succeed following the change.

10. Trumpet early successes to create momentum for change.

11. Continue to promote and reinforce the change after it has been launched.

12. Coach and support people in coming to grips with change after it has been implemented.

Chapter 3

Purpose

"Where there is no vision, the people perish"

Proverbs [12:18]

3.1 Direction

Being caught in a storm at sea teaches you the value of a compass. You may not be able to see exactly where you are going or steer a perfectly straight and steady course, but you can at least keep moving in the right general direction until the storm settles. So it is that a clear sense of purpose keeps you on track during turbulent times at work.

During periods of stability, when little is changing (a rarity these days), doing your job becomes relatively straightforward. You become accustomed to the constraints and trade-offs that need to be taken into account when making decisions. Problems take on familiar forms, as do their solutions. But introduce a significant change and the rulebook needs revising or even rewriting. Experience can no longer be relied upon. In these uncertain times a strong sense of purpose is indispensable.

If people understand and identify with an organisation's purpose they will more readily travel down a difficult and unfamiliar path to reach a destination they believe to be worthwhile. If this firm sense of purpose is supported by a strong set of guiding values then people can achieve extraordinary things in spite of the difficulties encountered along the way.

Whether or not an organisation and its people have a strong sense of purpose, it is vital to the success of any important change that leaders articulate repeatedly a clear purpose for the change and why it is worth making. This purpose should give people a strong sense of direction to help keep them motivated as they make the journey. The more closely aligned this purpose is to the purpose of the organisation the better, as misalignment between the two makes people feel as though they are being pulled in two different directions at the same time, causing confusion and making the journey a great deal harder to complete successfully.

3.2   Worthwhile work

Imagine you work as an operator in a factory and you are told by your foreman that an unusual order has come in that he wants you to complete. You need to cut hundreds of shapes out of wood. Another operator will have the task of painting them different colours. To begin with, you are asked to cut out squares which will be painted red. These squares need to be precisely 5 cm by 5 cm with smooth edges and corners, and the paint must be even and unblemished. You need to cut out the shapes using an electric hand saw and smooth the edges with an electric sander at a rate of over 200 a day, Five days a week, for a fortnight. You are paid a basic wage and a bonus based on the quantity and quality of your output. The work is quite fiddly at first and a number of the squares you produce are rejected as out of spec or because of imperfect paintwork.

After two weeks you are told to move on to producing wooden triangles to be painted yellow. A fortnight later it is blue semi-circles, then green rectangles and brown squares. After a couple of months you are a dab hand at cutting and smoothing wooden shapes. You find the work dull but the pay is ok and at least you enjoy your weekends. Eventually, you are told that you have produced enough wooden shapes and you are being moved on to an order for plastic shapes. You don't ask why.

How would you feel about this sort of work? Have you ever carried out repetitive and uninspiring tasks over a long period of time? How easy do you find it to stay motivated and focused on this kind of work?

One day, on the way to work, you are walking past a major public building and there in front of it is an enormous and beautiful picture. You stop in your tracks to admire it. It must be 50 feet tall. You notice other people stop and admire this great work of art that has miraculously appeared on the high street. After a while, you examine it a bit more closely and suddenly realise it is a giant mosaic made out of painted wooden shapes! As other passers-by stop to wonder at it you cannot remove a huge grin from your face. This is your handiwork.

Eventually, you continue your journey to work. But now there is lightness to your step and you are filled with a great sense of pride. The time at work seems to fly by. You work with extra care and begin to wonder what great use the plastic shapes you are cutting out will be put to.

This story demonstrates a simple truth, namely that any work becomes more engaging when there is a clear and useful purpose to it. Knowing that your effort is contributing to a greater good gives you a sense of pride and a reason for taking care to do a good job.

On the other hand, an absence of purpose is dispiriting. For example, think how you feel just after you have completed a major project or after working for weeks or months to meet a tough and important deadline. It is quite common to suffer "post-project blues" and feel a sense of deflation and listlessness for a day or two. It may seem odd that just as you expect to be delighted at achieving your goal and having the burden lifted from your shoulders you feel dissatisfied. In truth, a deadline gives you a strong sense of purpose and without it you can feel a little adrift. Similarly, after school exams students feel relieved that the weeks of revision and the nerve-jangling exam papers are over, but they can be surprised to find themselves at a loose end and slightly depressed in the days that follow as they lack that clear and present danger of failing their exams. At work, one of the great attractions of crisis management is the sense of unambiguous purpose associated with handling emergency situations.

Without a clear sense of purpose it is hard to stay motivated. It is all too easy to suspect that you are heading in the wrong direction and all your effort could simply be a waste of time. Yet in many enterprises people are not sure how they contribute to the overall purpose of the organisation. They often have a narrow view of their role, seeing it as a series of tasks rather than having an overall purpose or contributing to a wider goal. For instance, when working with meter readers at a utility company I asked them to explain the purpose of what they did. The answers they gave were along the lines that they were there to take accurate meter readings. It was only after some prompting that they began to view their job as providing the essential information upon which the entire company depended and that ultimately they helped provide clean and safe water to millions of people.

3.3 A great purpose

"We chose to go to the moon. We choose to go to the moon in this decade, and do the other things, not because they are easy but because they are hard; because that goal will serve to organize and measure the best of our energies and skills; because that challenge is one that we are willing to accept, one we are unwilling to postpone, and one which we intend to win — and the others, too."

John F Kennedy, 12th September 1962

During the space race between the Soviet Union and the USA in the 1960s, US President John F Kennedy visited NASA to see first hand the American preparations for space exploration. While he was touring the headquarter buildings he came across a man carrying a bucket and a mop. Kennedy asked him asked what he was doing. "Putting a man on the moon," was his simple reply.

When Nelson Mandela became President of the Republic of South Africa he talked of building a 'Rainbow Nation'. He was of course referring to the multi-ethnic nature of South Africa, which has 11 official languages. But the term 'Rainbow Nation' means more than this. It conjures up the beauty created by placing many contrasting colours together side by side. It uses the hopeful image of a rainbow to lift our thoughts up from the mundane and dares us to believe in something greater than ourselves despite the difficulties encountered day-to-day in learning to live harmoniously.

This vision played an important part in helping to create the belief that something extraordinary could be achieved in South Africa. It became symbolic of a miraculous transformation; the democratisation of a divided and embittered country without recourse to violence.

A great purpose is a powerful thing, but not everyone has the opportunity to build a new nation or put a man on the moon. However, every organisation has its part to play and has reasons to take pride in its contribution to society. Consider what different types of organisations might contribute:

- A pharmaceutical company – "We eliminate diseases from the world."

- A bank – "We help people achieve their dreams."
- A hospital – "We save lives."
- An insurance company – "We support you in times of disaster."
- A school – "We enable children to flourish."
- Cosmetics – "We help you look good and feel good."
- Beer – "We help you relax and enjoy time with your friends."
- Airlines – "We open up the world to you."

A strong purpose binds an organisation together in the pursuit of its goals. At best, it transcends the day-to-day, captures the imagination and gives people a sense of contributing to something greater than themselves. It challenges people to reach further than they might have thought possible to achieve something they can be proud of. It unleashes people's energy and creativity.

Take the example of the Body Shop which was launched in 1976 as a cosmetics retailer that banned animal testing on its products and now has over 2,100 stores in 55 countries. The ethos of the company, embodied by its founder Anita Roddick, was one of caring for the planet decades ahead of the evidence of global warming. It is not just a retailer, it is a champion of ethical practices in business and for the preservation of the planet. It attracts people who identify with its ethos as well its products. It doesn't just have staff and customers – it has loyal fans, which is a powerful thing in business.

Many organisations have Corporate Social Responsibility (CSR) programmes that give back to the community by raising money for charity or carrying out voluntary work. These are important and praiseworthy schemes that enable organisations to contribute to society as responsible "corporate citizens". However, they are no substitute for a grand purpose that touches everyone who comes into contact with an organisation and is truly taken to heart by its people.

A strong sense of purpose is vital to long-term organisational success. It binds people together in a common cause and helps inspire them to strive for difficult goals. A well crafted purpose provides a short-hand description for what needs to be done, simplifying decision-making and coordinating the efforts of hundreds or thousands of people. Without it an organisation can be easily blown off course or even destroyed the first time it faces real difficulties.

Like Moses leading the children of Israel through the desert for 40 years, it is an essential role of leaders to convey a steadfast vision of the Promised Land. This in turn needs to be supported by a set of enduring principles describing the rules and behaviours that underpin the way in which the journey should be made.

3.4 Guiding values

When you ask a child what they want to be when they grow up they will usually reply 'fireman' or 'nurse' or 'ballet dancer' or 'pilot'. It is a rare child indeed who would reply 'kind', 'generous', 'loved' or 'admired'. In the same way, most organisations are clear about what they want to achieve in terms of tangible goals but less so about how they want to *be*.

If an organisation's purpose is a guiding star that helps people navigate over great distances then an organisation's *values* are signposts that direct its people as to how the journey should be made. Do we want to win at all costs or to be a responsible citizen? Do we sell products to customers (a series of transactions) or do we serve them at a deeper level? Are we about high quality or low cost?

Many successful CEOs understand the benefit of investing time and effort in defining their values and engaging their staff in applying them in their every day working lives. This is based on the belief that a strong set of values helps unify an organisation and channel people's energy into the things that really matter. As an organisation grows, lines of communication become longer. Improvised cultures can develop in different parts of the organisation in the absence of any clear guidelines, so it becomes increasingly important to communicate a clear set of values

Even if not explicitly stated, every organisation has a set of values. They may simply be understood by people as "the way we do things around here" without anyone ever putting them into words or committing them to paper. Just coming into contact with an organisation will tell you how much they care about their customers. Do they take great pains to help you get what you want or are you just another person to be processed? Whatever the case, somewhere along the line each person has come to understand that great or indifferent service is par for the course. To some degree it is down to individuals to respond to the messages sent out by an organisation, but in the main it is up to leaders to embody and ingrain desired attitudes and behaviours.

3.5 Purposeful leadership

So why are purpose and values so important in the context of organisational change?

One clue comes from considering the characteristics of people widely regarded as great leaders. You might think of Winston Churchill, Gandhi, Nelson Mandela, Mother Theresa or Martin Luther King. Whether or not you admire these individuals it is undeniable that they were popular leaders in their time who brought about change or led people through times of great turbulence. Two things they had in common were an unerring sense of purpose and a clear set of beliefs which they communicated through words and deeds.

Such leadership is epitomised by the words of Abraham Lincoln in his speech at Gettysburg in 1863 honouring those who fought and died there during the American Civil War:

> "Four score and seven years ago our fathers brought forth on this Continent, a new nation, conceived in liberty and dedicated to the proposition that all men are created equal.
>
> Now we are engaged in a great civil war, testing whether that nation, or any nation so conceived and so dedicated, can long endure...It is rather for us to be here dedicated to the great task remaining before us – that from these honoured dead we take increased devotion to that cause for which they gave their last full measure of devotion – that we here highly resolve that these dead shall not have died in vain – that this nation, under God, shall have a new birth of freedom – and that government of the people, by the people, for the people, shall not perish from the earth."

In full, this speech contains only 266 words but remains the most famous speech in US history. It may appear to be about honouring fallen heroes but it is really about the enduring purpose and values of the United States of America as set out by its founding fathers. Its intention is to inspire people to sacrifice their comfort and even their lives for a grand and noble cause and an enduring set of beliefs. It is perhaps not surprising then that almost exactly 100 years later Martin Luther King, standing on the steps of the Lincoln Memorial in Washington, referred to the same values when calling for racial equality in America.

At a more everyday level, all enterprises have to overcome difficult circumstances and make bold changes at different points in their history. Events, such as the introduction of government regulation or the arrival of revolutionary new technology, may force a change in tactics or even a wholesale shift in direction. However, if people have a strong sense of their destination (organisational purpose) and the principles to be followed in getting there (organisational values), then it seems likely that this would make them more able to remain resolute in the face of dramatic changes, allowing the organisation to adapt and prosper in the long run. This feeling is borne out by the evidence.

In their book, *Built to Last*[1], James Collins and Jerry Porras demonstrate the value of ingraining a strong purpose and clear set of values within an organisation. The authors draw their conclusions from six years of research into what enables certain companies to outperform their competitors over a period of decades. These 'Visionary Companies' did not just survive and succeed over a long period of time; they outstripped competitors and the general stock market to a remarkable degree. Between 1926 and 1990 Collins and Porras found that Visionary Companies outperformed comparable companies (that were also successful businesses) by 6 to 1 in US stock market returns and the general stock market by 15 to 1.

Built to Last exploded a number of myths about what makes companies successful and established a set of characteristics that distinguished Visionary Companies from similar successful companies. The greatest correlation that Collins and Porras found with success was the existence of a 'Core Ideology' championed by leaders and internalised by staff. They describe Core Ideology as "Core Values + Purpose".

Many, if not all, of the Visionary Companies described in *Built to Last* have had their ups and downs, including near disastrous periods in their history. However, in the long run and despite great difficulties, they have remained successful. They have found the secret to longevity.

This is well summed up by Thomas J. Watson, Jr., former IBM Chief Executive, in explaining the role of core values (referred to as 'beliefs') in his 1963 booklet *A Business and its Beliefs* (quoted in *Built to Last*[1]):

"I believe the real difference between success and failure in a corporation can very often be traced to the question of how well the organization brings out the great energies and talents of its people. What does it do to help these people find common cause with each other? ... And how can it sustain this common cause and sense of direction through the many changes which take place from one generation to another? ... [I think the answer lies] in the power of what we all call beliefs and the appeal these beliefs have for its people....I firmly believe that any organisation in order to survive and achieve success, must have a sound set of beliefs on which it premises all its policies and actions. Next, I believe that the most important single factor in corporate success is faithful adherence to those beliefs."

Looking at things from the opposite end of the spectrum, organisations lacking a clear purpose and clear values certainly struggle with change.

Take the example of Marks and Spencer stores (M&S), a hugely successful retail business started in 1884 and the first retailer in the UK to achieve pre-tax profits of over £1bn in 1998. This company, much loved by its customers (at one time 80% of women's underwear in the UK was bought from M&S), went through a period of decline around the turn of the century. Pre-tax profits fell to £145m in 2001 and two Chief Executives left within three years.

At the end of 2004, a new Chief Executive, Stuart Rose (now Sir Stuart Rose), himself a former M&S man, began to turn the ship around. By 2007 it was widely acknowledged that M&S was once again a highly successful organisation. Pre-tax profits for the year ending March 2008 topped £1bn once again.

When Stuart Rose took up the helm at M&S, one thing he did was to return to what had made M&S so successful in the past. Prior to his arrival, there had been a number of years characterised at first by denial that there was a need to change and then by loss of direction. In the 1990s the marketplace changed dramatically. M&S had been a byword for quality and reliability, but now its competitors, such as Next, were able to undercut M&S on price and still deliver similar quality. Rather than looking for durability, customers were treating clothes as disposable. 'Fast Fashion' arrived on the scene led by organisations such as Zara of Spain who were able to respond rapidly to emerging trends by manufacturing on an 'as needed' basis, bringing in extra stock for lines that sold well and abandoning unpopular lines with very limited wastage. M&S, who had stood supreme in the market for so long, failed to anticipate these trends or even to react to lost market share. A new CEO arrived and attempted to move M&S into home furnishings rather than fixing its core clothing and food businesses. Internally, it launched a campaign known as "Be Free" which encouraged people to abandon the old shackles of a command and control culture and to become empowered. However, for an organisation built on 100 years of strong centralised leadership and procedure, it was a recipe for disaster and different areas of the business set off in different directions.

What Rose did was to keep it simple. He put the focus back on giving the customers what they wanted: great product, excellent customer service and an appealing environment in store. He also returned to the core values of Quality, Service, Value, Innovation and Trust that had made M&S great, while bringing them up to date. For instance, great product now meant 'regular newness' in store – i.e. a continuous flow of fresh new product and keeping up with fashion trends using the principles of Fast Fashion.

In terms of setting out a clear sense of purpose, Rose also kept it very simple. 2004/05 was dedicated to 'Focus' on the core business and stemming losses. 2005/06 was about 'Drive', i.e. improving product, customer service and the environment in store. The catchword for 2006/07 was 'Broaden' and is evidenced by M&S's ambitious ongoing expansion abroad.

Whilst this is a great simplification of the M&S story, which was of course not without its trials and tribulations, looked at as a whole it is a classic example of a great company regaining its sense of purpose and values after having lost its way for some time. It illustrates the power of a clear purpose and set of values in bringing about change.

In *Built to Last,* Collins and Porras also discovered an important lesson about change. Visionary Companies continually drive progress through experimentation and innovation but they never let go of their Core Ideology (Purpose + Core Values) while doing so. It is this Core Ideology that provides people with a firm foundation and makes them resilient to change. It allows them to respond quickly and successfully to changes in the environment whilst holding onto what has made them successful in the past and maintaining an unerring sense of purpose.

3.6   A purpose for change

When an organisation embarks on a major change a clear purpose for the change is an essential ingredient for success. This purpose should be clearly and passionately communicated by someone at the executive level, preferably the Chief Executive, and linked to the overall purpose of the organisation.

A well defined purpose for change helps inspire people, creates simplicity and focuses people's effort. Inspiration may be in the form of a challenging goal that goes beyond simply what will be changed. For instance, the purpose of implementing a new call centre system could be defined as "To install the new call centre system to greatly reduce the number of inbound calls missed". Alternatively, it might be "Never miss a call". Most likely, this second definition is beyond people's expectations and motivates them to think more widely and creatively about what they need to do beyond simply installing a new system to eliminate lost calls. It is simple, unambiguous and more inspiring than "greatly reduce missed calls". It also simplifies decision-making, as anything that does not contribute to eliminating all missed calls can be ignored or done away with.

As explained in Chapter 2, a clear purpose for change also provides a degree of certainty during uncertain times. We can feel confident of our destination even if we are not entirely clear about how we are going to get there. A well-crafted purpose provides a rallying call, cuts through complexity and focuses the efforts of maybe hundreds or thousands of people. However, this is only one piece in the overall jigsaw puzzle of change. Too often it is imagined that simply pointing towards the objective and shouting "charge!" is enough to motivate the troops and that if anyone chooses to stay in the trenches rather than taking to the battlefield, it's their problem, not the organisation's. Organisation change is not simply a matter of getting people revved up to charge at some objective, it requires a change to ingrained attitudes and beliefs. Therefore the purpose for change must reflect the changes in these attitudes and beliefs required for the vision of change to be achieved.

Where there is no clarity of purpose, large-scale change can easily run into trouble. For starters, some people will inevitably rail against anything that appears to be change for change's sake. Others will get lost in the complexity of the change, spending too long prevaricating over decisions in the absence of clear direction. As a result, major projects can drift and ultimately get killed off when they lose their momentum and are no longer seen as a priority (especially where benefits take a while to accrue).

The flipside of a good purpose for change is the risk of doing nothing. In other words, if the current situation is sufficiently perilous or painful it may encourage people to see change as salvation from their troubles (often referred to as a *burning platform*). For instance, call centre staff are much more likely to welcome a new call centre system if they are losing out on monthly bonuses due to the high numbers of missed calls. So it pays to spell out the dangers of standing still. However, it is important not to make the mistake of assuming too much. Yes, people would like bigger bonuses, but they will still have to put up with the inevitable disruption associated with the introduction of a new system. On top of that, can they be sure that it will work any better than the last system or that it won't work so well that they lose their jobs? So you still have your work cut out even when a change appears at first to be nothing but good news. The idea that things are so bad that people have no choice but to change is a false one. It may encourage more people to come on board, but there will always be some who will not budge until they are up to their chins in floodwater.

An excellent example of a purpose for change is the target set by Marks and Spencer (M&S), to become carbon neutral by 2012. This vision, known as Plan A ("because there is no Plan B") was announced by its CEO, Stuart Rose, in January 2007 amidst great publicity, making it the first major UK organisation to set such a target.

M&S have set themselves a very ambitious goal, which by its very nature will challenge people to devise innovative solutions and require everyone to play their part. It is also a very simple statement of intent that leaders in every part of the company can easily translate into goals for their part of the business. As a result, it is easy for everyone to achieve clarity and a clear sense of how they can contribute to the delivery of Plan A. Figure 3.1 below illustrates just a few of the objectives that *might* fall out of Plan A in different parts of the business.

A further important feature of Plan A is that it is not simply a set of initiatives but a brand. As a result, it does not impose limits on activity and can take on a life of its own. It also becomes shorthand for a great many different activities, simplifying communication and focusing activity within the company. Branding your change helps position it not just as another project that must be completed but also as a major shift in attitudes and behaviours.

At M&S the purpose of Plan A is unambiguous. This empowers people at M&S to take action as they see fit as long as it supports the overall goal. It also gives them room to respond flexibly to changing circumstances and reduces the likelihood of people wasting effort pursuing activities that do not support the overall purpose.

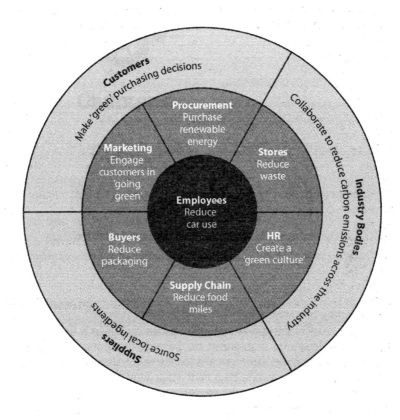

Figure 3.1 Plan A – Possible objectives for different areas of M&S or for different external stakeholders in support of the objective of achieving Carbon Neutral status by 2012

3.7   Alignment of purpose and values

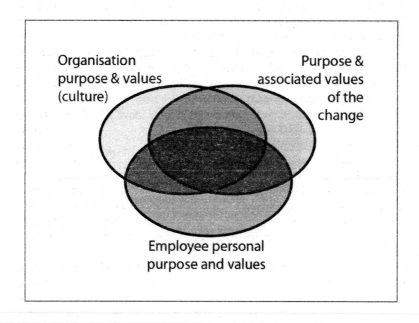

Figure 3.2 Alignment between purpose and values of an
organisation, its employees and an organisational change

There is an important relationship between an organisation's purpose and values and the purpose and associated values of any major change it embarks upon. If the purpose of the change is clearly aligned with the overall purpose of the organisation (i.e. there is a large overlap between the top two rings in Figure 3.2) then it is easy and helpful for leaders to be able to point out this alignment and demonstrate that the change is all part of the 'grand plan' and not a great diversion from the current path. The bridge that must be built between the present and the future is not too long or too difficult to build. People will be more tolerant of an incomplete picture of how change will be brought about if they know they are still heading towards a familiar destination. This is a tremendous boon when, as is inevitable, plans change, making the road to success a circuitous one.

Of course, it helps if your overall organisational purpose and values are already well understood within your organisation. If not, you will need to improvise by building your change on what people at least *perceive* to be the purpose and values of your organisation.

There is, of course, a danger when organisations embark on fundamental change, such as a new strategy or a merger, that the purpose of the change will conflict with the existing purpose and values of the organisation. A fundamental change in strategy can lead to 'organisational schizophrenia' as people are dragged in different directions by incompatible or contradictory priorities. This in turn leads high degrees of stress and a drop in morale driving down performance. So if the change you are undertaking requires a radical departure from the current culture you need to make a big investment of time and effort in bridging the gap between where you are and where you want to be (using all the methods described in this book). Getting stuck half way between where you are now and some desired future state can be far worse than not changing at all. In the words of Benjamin Disraeli "The most dangerous strategy is to jump a chasm in two leaps."

The research on which James Collins and Jerry Porras based their book *Built to Last* showed that one strong indicator of a Visionary Company was a 'Cult-Like Culture'. In other words, a condition for long-term organisational success is a strong alignment between employees' personal purpose and values and the purpose and values of the organisation that they work for.

In Figure 3.2, the bottom ring represents the purpose and values of the individuals within an organisation. According to Collins and Porras's research we would want there to be a great deal of overlap between this and the purpose and values of the organisation. Where the overlap is small, people find themselves at odds with the organisation they work for and generally unhappy at work. That is why many successful organisations seek out individuals who share similar values to themselves. For instance, the recruitment process for one UK supermarket includes putting potential recruits out on the shop floor to see if they are have a natural bent for customer service (one of the company's core values).

Major change can put people at odds with the organisation that they work for. A policeman who wants to arrest criminals may find himself sat behind a desk, an ambitious go-getter may find herself in a flat organisation structure with nowhere to go and a computer geek may find himself having to work directly with customers. These people will try to escape to a new situation inside or outside of their current organisation or else they will stay put and suffer frustration and deliver poor results.

Introducing a major change is easiest when the purpose and values of the organisation are aligned well with those of its employees as well as those associated with the proposed change i.e. the central shaded area in Figure 3.2 is as large as possible. So starting off with employees who are already well aligned with their organisation's purpose and values gives you a better chance of succeeding with any given change. Another way of putting this is that the greater the alignment between an organisation and its people, the more adaptable that organisation is to change. No wonder then that Collins and Porras discovered that long term organisational success correlated with a cult-like culture.

When an organisation makes a fundamental change to its strategy it can come into conflict with its own purpose and values as well as those of its people.

Take the example of a large US bank that made its name over many decades as a bastion of responsible investment through conservative management of its clients' funds. Then one day a new CEO decides that the company needs to push ahead with an aggressive strategy of expansion into Europe through acquisition as well as organic growth. The result was a case of organisational schizophrenia.

On the one hand, there was a desire to venture out into new markets and new cultures, to experiment and make bold decisions. On the other hand, there was a leadership team used to pondering new ideas at length to weigh up the pros and cons and to select the most prudent course of action. Those charged with driving expansion in Europe were stuck in the middle between a centralised, consensus-orientated decision-making machine and a fast-growing heterogeneous organisation that needed quick and decisive leadership.

At the same time, one of the newly acquired businesses in Europe was suffering its own personality disorder. It too had a highly conservative culture and valued its long-standing approach to developing personalised client relationships based on intimate knowledge and trust. People at every level felt threatened by changes being introduced by the new parent company such as a new computer system for tracking customer communication and new requirements to report progress both to the US and to functional heads dotted around Europe. They felt that these changes signalled a more bureaucratic approach and an end to their tradition of personalised service.

The US bank had not taken the time to explain to the people in their newly acquired European organisation that far from wanting them to change their ways they also valued building long-term client relationships based on trust and that new technology was merely a tool for enabling this process. Ironically, the parent company was so sure of its own purpose and values that they took it for granted that its new employees would somehow absorb them by osmosis. It was only when they faced near-revolt by staff that they worked with them to uncover the causes of their concern and began to dispel the misconceptions that had gained credence in the absence of any open dialogue.

When two organisations merge, it is often the case that the cultures of the merging organisations differ greatly. Opting for one or other culture to become the new dominant culture runs the risk of alienating a whole section of the population and is often at the root of the many problems associated with mergers and acquisitions. Where possible, it is better to start again from scratch and create a new single unified purpose and set of values that both populations can sign up to. Where this is not possible, then attention must be paid to inducting the people into their new organisation as if they had just been recruited, setting out the purpose and core values and helping them understand what has remained unchanged for them and what they must now leave behind.

For any major change, understanding how far a change is shifting you from your existing purpose and values helps you identify the cultural issues that you will need to tackle to be successful. It also helps ensure that people have an accurate view of what needs to change and reassurance about what will remain the same.

Summary

During periods of great change, an organisation's purpose and core values help people maintain a sense of direction. It is up to leaders, especially those at the top of an organisation, to convey a purpose for the change, linked to the organisation's overall purpose, which inspires people and provides the confidence to embark on an uncertain journey.

Leaders should:

1. Reiterate the organisation's purpose and core values to help increase the organisation's ability to adapt to change.

2. Define and repeatedly communicate a compelling purpose for change.

3. Spell out the dangers of standing still.

4. Explain how the change supports the organisation's overall purpose.

5. Brand the change (as M&S have done with Plan A) to help bring it to life and to engage people's energy and ingenuity in making it successful.

6. Be aware of any perceived or real differences between the purpose of the change and the purpose and values of the organisation and its people. Anticipate and address any problems that might arise as a result of these differences using the techniques described in this chapter.

7. Explain to people what will remain the same as well as what will change as a result of the organisational change.

Chapter 4

Control

"When the best leader's work is done, the people say
'We did it ourselves'."

Lao Tse

4.1   School dinners

In 2006, the BBC screened a television series following the exploits of TV chef Jamie Oliver and his attempts to improve the healthiness of school meals in the UK. The series revealed how school children were being fed large quantities of highly processed, fatty, salty, fried food and went on to try to change the habits of cooks and children alike by introducing healthy school meals. At a time when the media was already full of stories of increasing childhood obesity and youngsters spending their lives playing computer games instead of taking regular exercise, journalists were quick to latch on to what Jamie was doing and it rapidly became a headline story. Indeed, so much attention was generated that government politicians were soon meeting Jamie Oliver in public to voice their concerns on the matter and, after some prevarication, eventually pledged government support and money for improved school meals.

However, this was by no means the whole story. It was not just a case of a fearless young chef exposing the harm we were inflicting on young children, bringing a government to its senses and everyone living happily ever after. This was a fundamental shift in something close to children's hearts, namely what they ate for lunch. It was an attempt to end their love affair with junk food, epitomized by fried processed turkey pieces, known as 'Turkey Twizzlers'.

As any parent knows, persuading a child to eat something they don't want to eat is one of the toughest jobs there is. Not only that; there was the issue of low-paid, undertrained dinner ladies (school cooks) on a very tight budget being asked to come up with recipes that were interesting and healthy when they were used to taking processed food out of plastic packets or tins and boiling or frying it. And all of this was before the parents themselves got involved.

The story of Jamie's School Dinners, as the series was called, is a classic tale of change and how people respond to new situations. In particular, it highlights one of the basic themes of change, which is the human need for control over their environment and the things that affect their lives. More of this later.

4.2 Control

Since the dawn of civilisation, we have sought to control our environment. In modern cities we are kept warm in winter, air-conditioned in summer, protected from many of the worst diseases and can eat summer fruits in the dead of winter. Yes, we are still prone to natural disasters and are now under threat from global warming, but we exercise huge control over our world; we even have the power to annihilate it.

In our personal lives we also like to exercise a good deal of control. We may not all have a burning need to be in charge or to make all the important decisions. We are not all "control freaks", but to varying degrees we all like a sense of autonomy and the ability to run our lives the way we choose, whether inside work or outside of it. Anyone who has worked for a boss who is always looking over their shoulder, checking up on them and generally "micro-managing" will know the sense of irritation this brings and the feeling that one is not trusted to do a good job. In the worst cases, people give up thinking for themselves when it becomes too difficult to second guess what their boss wants. So a healthy balance of control is vital to ensuring that people can make a full contribution at work.

But there is another school of thought born out of the Industrial Revolution and the arrival of mass production. It is rarely explicitly stated but at its root is an assumption that people can be thought of as cogs in an industrial machine and can be managed and controlled like any other piece of equipment. We see evidence of this everywhere. Think, for example, of the term 'Human Resources'. Human Resources (HR) professionals are, generally-speaking, the people that look after people, providing benefits, ensuring well-being and helping them to develop their skills. But the very name Human Resources implies that humans are simply resources, like machinery or fuel, to be fed into the production line. So even the department most associated with people's welfare (HR) has a name that suggests quite the opposite.

Then there is the curse of the organisation structure chart. A benign thing, you might think, that explains how an organisation is ordered into departments and reporting lines to achieve its goals. However, looked at another way, it is a blueprint for control that can lead people into thinking of an organisation as the sum of its reporting lines and the power relationships between different people. It encourages some executives to view their workforce like pieces on a chessboard and leads them to wonder how better results might be achieved if only people were shifted to different positions.

No wonder then that many of the best and most successful organisations have thrown their structure charts in the bin.

Take, for instance, W L Gore & Associates, makers of Gore-Tex weatherproof clothing, which was ranked number 1 in "The Sunday Times Top 100 UK Companies to Work For" for four years on the trot from 2004 to 2007.[1]

American Scientist Bill Gore, who founded the company with his wife Vieve in 1958, believed a non-hierarchical environment would allow creative minds to flourish. Hence there are no job descriptions or titles, no structure chart, no managers, just leaders who make up about half the 454 staff. Everyone is an Associate and knows what they have to do to make the organisation successful and they have the autonomy to get on with doing it. They are paid according to the contribution they make to the organisation, with colleagues helping decide on their pay. Asking for help is seen as a sign of strength and the few people in who occupy what might be considered 'senior' positions are responsible for supporting other Associates in achieving their goals.

In this chapter, we will scrutinize the critical role of control during change. In particular, the important choices leaders must make about taking charge of change or ceding control to others.

4.3 Feeling powerless

"Let me appeal to your sense of doing things my way."

In Douglas Adams's 'A Hitchhiker's Guide to the Galaxy', the earth is demolished to make way for a galactic superhighway. A brief announcement is made to the people of earth giving them 24 hours notice to leave their planet before the galactic equivalent of the bulldozers move in. This is the final comeuppance for all Earthly government bureaucrats who have ridden roughshod over local people's wishes, demolishing countryside in the name of the motorcar. It is also the ultimate example of unthinking centrally-controlled bureaucracy.

We have all, at one time or another, been hugely frustrated by someone, with little apparent insight into our world, making decisions on our behalf. National governments, by their very nature, make decisions every day affecting millions of people often without a real understanding of the practical consequences to individuals and their everyday lives. Even local government officials, who are meant to be in touch with the people they serve, make decisions about building roads and closing down schools that have whole communities up in arms.

In the 1960s and 1970s the UK government's solution to providing low-cost housing for the poor was to demolish swathes of Victorian terraced housing and replace it with high-rise apartment blocks. These marvellous new buildings that made use of the latest construction materials and building technology were monuments to progress and triumphs of modern architecture. In reality, they turned out to have one major drawback – they were terrible places to live. Lifts broke down. Concrete walkways became home to muggers and drug dealers. People piled on top of each other did not have the space to create community spirit or for children to play out in the open. Unsurprisingly, there was a great deal of nostalgia for life in the old Victorian terraces.

Nowadays, more enlightened developers and local councils spend time consulting with the local community to understand their needs and how they would like to live. Housing is now better understood in human terms – the need to build communities, support families and treat people as individuals. The important lesson is that people are not objects but intelligent citizens with a clear understanding of their own needs who must be engaged in decisions that affect their lives. Any other approach is bound to fail.

The same is true in the workplace. Just substitute national government for head office. Think of a time when a proclamation has been issued by someone at head office that seems to bear no relation to the situation you find yourself in on the ground. For example, it is close to financial year-end and you are steaming towards your annual target. Something has gone wrong somewhere else in your organisation so it is now decreed that your targets have been raised by 5%. You then have the unenviable task of explaining to your team that despite a weakening market for your goods or services and the enormous effort they have made to deliver what was agreed at the start of the year, the goalposts have just been moved.

Seemingly arbitrary decisions by those in authority generate two forms of negative reaction; fight or flight. Fight involves open hostility or, more likely, covert opposition. Flight involves people opting out mentally (putting in the minimum effort to get by) or simply leaving.

4.4   The Whitehall Study

In 1967, a now famous study, known as The Whitehall Study[2], into the lives of 18,000 male British civil servants was launched. It tracked civil servants over 25 years. One of its most significant findings came from an analysis of the correlation between the occurrence of heart disease and level of seniority in the civil service. The results were surprising.

The received wisdom at the time was that people at the top of an organisation, with higher levels of responsibility and the burden of leadership and decision-making, endured the highest levels of stress. It was also known that higher levels of stress correlated closely with higher incidence of heart disease and death. However, what this study indicated was quite the reverse. People in the lower echelons of the civil service suffered far higher mortality rates than those at the top (the rate for those at the lowest levels was 4 times higher than those in the highest levels!). These results flew in the face of received wisdom and when the results were published it was thought by many that there was something peculiar about male civil servants, making them an exception to the rule. However, later studies across a range of organisations proved that the results for the civil service were typical of people across the national and international workforce. In other words, it was tougher at the bottom or the middle than at the top. Why were people in less high-powered jobs suffering greater degrees of stress?

This question forced people to think again about the conditions at work giving rise to stress. The results of the Whitehall Study and the second Whitehall Study (Whitehall II[2]), initiated in 1985, and which continues even today, are illustrated in Figures 4.1 and 4.2. Whitehall II included female as well as male civil servants and asked people a series of questions about their working lives, which included the level of control they had in their roles. As can be seen from the graphs in Figure 4.1 and 4.2, the incidence of Coronary Heart Disease (CHD) is strongly reduced for people in more senior grades of the civil service and also reduced the more control people felt they had at work. If there is a great deal of pressure on a person to deliver results at work but they have little control over things that influence those results it leads to high levels of stress. If you are working in a call centre, for instance, answering hundreds of customer calls and under pressure from your boss to deal with customer queries quickly and effectively, yet the information you need to do this is sitting in a computer system that is unreliable and very hard to navigate, then you are going to find your work highly stressful.

Think of the manager caught between a corporate decree to increase targets by 5% and a team that has pulled out all the stops only to find that they are going to fail because the bar has suddenly been raised. If this doesn't cause stress it is because the manager no longer cares or has learnt to block it out (neither of which is conducive to success at work). But it is even worse for the team members working for the manager who may have little or no idea why the targets have been raised by 5% and very little opportunity to influence the decision while having little hope of delivering on the new targets. Even a 3% uplift would seem like failure.

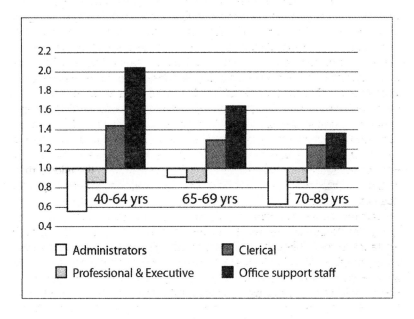

Figure 4.1 Death rate and employment grade over 25 year period in men. Death rate is relative to the average which is set at 1.

Note: Administrators ('Admin') are in the top civil service grades and Office Support staff ('Other') are in the lowest civil service grades. Death rates are in comparison to the average across the civil service i.e. Administrators aged 40-64 have about half the average mortality rate, whereas Office Support staff mortality is about twice the average. Hence there is about a fourfold difference between the top and bottom grade.

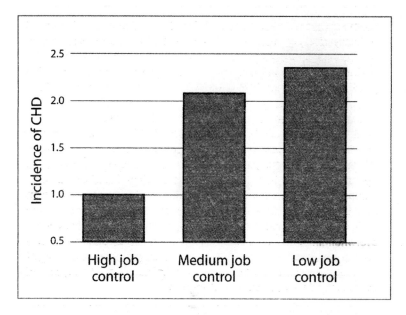

Figure 4.2 Self-reported job control and Coronary Heart Disease incidence. Adjusted for age, sex, length of follow-up, effort-reward balance, grade, coronary risk factors and negative affect

For a simple day-to-day example, remember how it feels when your computer crashes or equipment fails just as you are approaching a tight deadline. It is the loss of control that leads to feelings of stress, putting a strain on your heart which can eventually lead to CHD.

What this tells us about change is clear – combine the psychological demands of change with a lack of control, and people will suffer stress. This may manifest itself in a variety of ways from anxiety to anger and inevitably has a damaging effect on performance at work.

It is not just centralised authority that is guilty of ignoring how people might be affected by their decisions. It is a trap that we can all wander into. Inexperienced project teams, charged with introducing change, are especially vulnerable.

I came across a good example of this at a retailer of a global brand of luxury clothing. They were implementing a new enterprise-wide computer system. An internal team was set up to amend the business processes to increase efficiency and ensure that working practices fitted smoothly and efficiently with the new IT system. Some months into the process, the Head of Organisation Development complained that the team had disappeared into a black hole. They could be seen from time to time in meeting rooms drawing up process flow diagrams and brainstorming all sorts of interesting looking things but little was known about what they were up to. Eventually, they began to present their solutions to large groups of startled people who proceeded to pick holes in their plan and generally declare their work a failure. The project came perilously close to being abandoned by executives in the face of the overwhelmingly negative reaction it had received, and it was only after an extended period of argument, negotiation and reworking of ideas that people started to accept how things should be organised for the introduction of the new IT system.

It is all too easy to get so engrossed in designing a change that you begin to take other people for granted – it can come as a bit of a shock when those people react badly to the change when it is presented as a done deal.

4.5 The tale of the Turkey Twizzler

Now back to our TV chef and Jamie's School Dinners. Jamie Oliver began by working closely with the Dinner Ladies at one particular school, devising ways of producing healthy meals on a tight budget. At the same time he began to educate children in the school about the amount of oil they were consuming with their fried food.

Things did not run smoothly. The Dinner Ladies had had very little training in the past and were daunted by the prospect of cooking rice and vegetables instead of chips and processed Turkey Twizzlers. They were also rightly doubtful that children would welcome a change of diet.

The initial results were poor. A number of children refused point blank to eat the strange new healthy food, leaving it on their plates or opting for sandwiches over cooked meals. But over time more and more kids tried out the new dishes and became converts. Eventually, the majority had made the move away from unhealthy eating. However, several weeks into the experiment there was still a small group of pupils who steadfastly refused to be won over. What Jamie did next was to switch tactics. He took a group of kids who would have absolutely nothing to do with healthy eating and gave them a lesson is how to cook healthy meals. Children who would never have dreamt of eating a salad were taught how to prepare one from scratch and had fun in the process. This was enough to tip the balance and encourage almost all of them to begin to try healthy eating.

So the answer is to "Get people into the kitchen" – i.e. give them knowledge and control over their environment. If you simply present them with the finished dish there is a good chance that they will turn their noses up at it.

Jamie Oliver's success in one school was just the beginning of the story and there were several twists in the tale still to come. The next step was to spread the gospel of healthy eating to other schools and to the rest of the country. Jamie was faced with training a legion of dinner ladies from different schools, all nervous and highly sceptical about the prospect of success.

One thing Jamie did have in his favour was a success story at his first school and perhaps more importantly, he had recruited the head cook, Nora, from that school to preach the gospel to her peers. Nora was able to tell them that she had been as sceptical as they were in the beginning and, whilst it was not going to be easy, she had learnt from her personal experience that it would work out in the end. This highlights an important principle in bringing about change which is that peer-to-peer communication is the most powerful way of getting your message across. People trust people like themselves to give the good and the bad news and they like to hear about what needs to be done from someone who has been there and done it. Nora therefore played an important part in winning over this crucial group of people who would be spearheading the next phase of the campaign.

Meanwhile, Jamie used the power of the media to generate publicity for the cause and to create a groundswell of public opinion in favour of improving school meals. Pretty soon he was face to face with government ministers, putting them on the spot about the health of the nation and after some excuses and prevarication the government eventually conceded that they would make to the necessary investment to deliver improvements across the board.

But this was still not the end of the story. In the following months, as processed meat and fried chips were being removed from school dining halls there was a backlash. Television and newspapers were reporting on an unprecedented new phenomenon. Parents were arriving outside schools at lunchtime laden with packs of fried fish, hamburgers and chips and handing them out through the school railings to throngs of hungry children (see Figure 4.3). Something, it seemed, had gone wrong.

When these parents were interviewed they expressed their anger at the new school meals being forced on their children, who, as a result, were going hungry through the day. They were not going to stand by while their children went without a decent meal and so they were fighting back with burgers and chips.

It is surely the most basic duty of a parent to ensure that their child is fed and yet they had not been consulted anywhere along the line about the strange new meals. In the face of such a seeming lack of respect there was an inevitable backlash.

One important lesson from this story is the need to understand who all of your stakeholders are. It may not just be people inside your organisation. Quite often customers and suppliers are an integral part of any change programme. If, for instance, you wish to reduce the carbon footprint of your organisation, you will need suppliers to provide you with 'green' products. Likewise, customers may need to be engaged in the process so they are not put off when your goods and services are delivered in different 'greener' ways.

Figure 4.3 Mothers outside Rawmarsh Comprehensive School in Rotherham, South Yorkshire, take orders for fried food through the school railings, September 2006[3]

4.6 Not invented here

I was once part of a team of consultants that descended on a motorway construction site with the unenviable task of increasing output. Try to imagine what happens when you explain to the foreman of a road-building gang that you might be able to help him lay tarmac 40% faster. You might think he would shake you warmly by the hand with an eager grin on his face and ask, "When can we get started?"

What happened in my case was he looked me up and down with an air of amusement mixed with contempt and explained that he and the bloke standing next to him had over 40 years of road-laying experience between them and if it were possible, they would have done it already. His boss was more subtle. He said, "I'll be interested in seeing how you do that." By "interested" he meant "it will never work" and by "you" he meant "do not expect any help from us – in fact, we will be trying to block you every step of the way."

Quite apart from feeling understandably sceptical that an outsider might be able to radically improve the way tarmac is laid, there was also the implication that we thought they had been "doing it the wrong way" for many years. They were hardly going to admit to this without feeling pretty foolish. On top of that, their sense of control over what they did and how they did it was under threat. This is quite apart from the fact that for the labourers there was a strong disincentive to finish a job faster, as many of them could simply be laid off until another building contract started up. So it is not surprising that some people took great pains to find reasons why our proposed approach would not work, questioning the data we had collected and blaming inefficiencies on exceptional circumstances such as equipment failure. Others quietly got on with undermining the whole thing – for example, by bringing extra trucks and machinery into the areas that we were assessing in order to boost apparent efficiency before implementation of any change.

The construction industry is not a special case. It is true that you are more likely to end up with face-to-face confrontation on a construction site than in many other industries, but the underlying response to change being brought in from the outside is the same. People resent feeling like a pawns in a game – victims of change whose opinions can simply be ignored. It makes them feel undervalued and disrespected. In the case of the motorway construction project, it took a concerted effort over a long period of time to get people involved and actively contributing to the efficiency improvement effort before they started to become less sceptical and to take ownership for the required changes.

Change imposed form the outside, by its very nature, can set people against one another. When people are presented with a ready-made solution to a problem, their natural response is to begin to test it out in their minds. They check it for errors and loopholes and they begin to ask questions. The people who have built the solution finds themselves being cross-examined and may become defensive, especially if they do not have all the answers, and start to lose credibility. There is a feeling of "us" and "them", especially where the project team has done little to engage the general population prior to unveiling their plans. Concern can turn into resentment and resentment into conflict.

All of this can be avoided, or at least minimised, by giving people control. If, for instance, you involve people in solving a problem, they feel that their views are being respected and they build a sense of ownership for the solution. As a result, they will have little trouble with endorsing the solution when it is presented. Better still, they may even present it themselves. Another helpful approach is to present "ideas for discussion" rather than "the solution". This is not as effective as actively involving people, but it can be enough to ensure that people feel part of a dialogue. If they feel they have helped to build the solution they will be less inclined to spend their time trying to pick it apart.

Rather than sitting people at the back of the bus and not telling them where they are going, put people at the wheel of the bus or at least let them sit up front and read the map. You cannot always involve them in deciding where they are going but you can engage them in plotting the route to get there. In addition, tapping into as many people's opinions and ideas as is possible increases your chances of arriving at the right destination.

In the case of controversial changes, like those that involve redundancies, the question of involving people is a sensitive one. However, keeping people in the dark is not the answer. The fall-out is not just with the people who find themselves out of a job, but with the people left behind who may feel that an implicit bond of trust between employer and employee has been broken. This loss of trust can only be avoided by working openly with people. They need to be able to come to their own conclusions about the tough decisions that sometimes need to be taken when, for instance, there is a downturn in the market.

4.7　Increasing people's level of control

The diagram in Figure 4.4 below illustrates how 'ownership' of change increases with increasing levels of control. It provides a useful reference

for thinking about the level of control different stakeho\
change you are leading and what you could do to maximise
increase the probability that change will be accepted and add

When planning how to give people control over their ow\
should start by identifying all of the important players in \
initiative. Forget an important group and you can end u\
equivalent of angry parents thrusting fish and chips through \ ~~,,ool
railings undermining everything you are trying to achieve. As well as those
directly affected by the change, there are other, less obvious groups such
as customers, suppliers or senior people within your own organisation with
a peripheral connection to what you are doing. If you are instigating a
major change, it may have reverberations in totally unexpected areas of
the business. For instance, re-structuring one part of an organisation will
send the rumour mill into overdrive, and before you know it people on the
other side of the world with no connection to what is happening will be
worrying about job security.

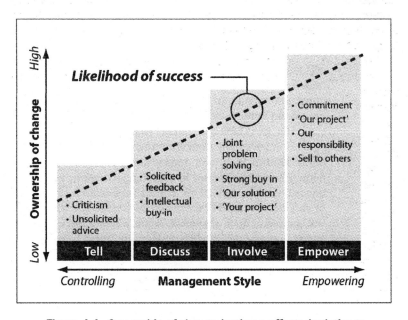

**Figure 4.4 Ownership of change by those affected relative to
management style (controlling versus empowering). Based on
Tannenbaum-Schmidt's Continuum of Leader Behaviour[4]**

take a look in turn at each of the four levels of control illustrated in Figure 4.4.

1. Tell (one-way communication)

One-way communication is the bare minimum level of control you can give to people. It is fine for those on the periphery of a major change, but not for those in the middle of it, unless it is a precursor to much deeper involvement. Merely telling people about a change that is going to affect them deeply demonstrates little respect for their feelings and their views. It generates understanding but very little ownership of the change. It is possible that it will give rise to resentment and feelings of "them and us". It may lead to negative behaviours such as picking holes in your proposals and looking for ways to undermine them. However, if you are smart and use all the media at your disposal (such as internal newsletters, the intranet and internal forums) you can create a campaign that goes beyond awareness and starts to create buy in through, for instance, publicising early successes and publishing Frequently Asked Questions. But if you are to succeed in your endeavour, a good media campaign should only be one component of your approach.

2. Discuss (two-way communication)

Two-way communication gives people a voice, allows them to question what is going to be done and, through discussion, start to rationalise the situation and to feel comfortable with it. To be effective, it needs to involve real dialogue. It is not simply a matter of asking people for their questions at the end of a presentation to a mass audience. Rather, it is about giving people time and space to explore the change, discuss its implications and begin to picture the new reality. One effective technique is to involve people in a series of small group discussions about each of the major areas of the change, brainstorming issues and ideas which can then be collated and presented back to a larger audience. This is more like consultation than presentation, and once again will enhance the quality of your solution as well as helping to get people on board.

In some ways, training is just an intense form of two-way communication, but it is often undervalued as an instrument of change. It represents a golden opportunity to engage a captive audience and bring them on board. Whilst it is clearly important to train people in new skills and methods you can achieve far more than this in the classroom or in a workshop. While giving people a chance to try out new methods, you can expose them to new attitudes and new ways of thinking. You can spell out (or people can work out for themselves) what will be expected of them once the change has taken place, putting them in command of the situation and increasing the likelihood they will adopt the new methods.

I worked with Sainsbury's Supermarkets for over three years starting at the end of 1999 to help them to set up and run an efficiency improvement team focused on driving cost out of their products (through things like better packaging, efficient transport, streamlined processing and improved supplier terms). We made decent headway in the first year as we worked with buyers, supply chain personnel and suppliers to eliminate waste despite a good deal of inertia and even opposition. The turning point came when we were asked by the trading directors to train all of their people in the efficiency improvement techniques that we were using, which is what we duly did over the following months.

Almost immediately, we saw an increase in cost savings. By the time we had trained all of the buyers savings took off like a rocket. This was not because each buyer we had trained rushed back to work and streamlined their supply chain (though a few did) but because now everyone we were working with understood the methods being used and no longer felt threatened by them (or by us). Suddenly, we found ourselves pushing at an open door.

We enjoyed active support from a trading team knowledgeable enough to spot improvement opportunities on our behalf and who actively encouraged us to get involved with their products. We also benefited from converting senior managers and executives to the cause by training them directly or training some of their most trusted direct reports. We moved from saving millions of pounds to tens of millions and eventually, picked up a 2003 National Training Award to boot.

This example demonstrates the tremendous benefits you can achieve from giving people a sense of control over their situation rather than making them feel like victims of external interference.

3. Involve

Involving people directly in bringing about change is a great way of harnessing people's energy and ingenuity in support of change. In general, it is only possible to fully involve a small proportion of people in your change project. There are a number of ways of doing this such as co-opting people into the project team, involving people in design workshops to help shape the change initiative and getting them to implement the change in their part of the organisation. All of these methods draw people towards the centre of the change, giving them a sense of control and a stake in its success, leading to higher levels of ownership.

Choosing who to involve in the change is an important decision. Enthusiasts for change are useful allies who can be relied upon to dedicate themselves to making the change a success. However, it is important to identify people who are well known within the organisation, as they can have a disproportionate effect in convincing others to come on board. There is also the question of sceptics who typically lag behind in accepting new ideas. Bringing them on board and converting them to the cause sends out a powerful signal to others that this change should be taken seriously. However, it would be counter-productive to fill your project team with sceptics.

4. Empower

People with direct responsibility or accountability for defining and implementing a change will quickly identify with the project and regard its success or failure as their success or failure. Put people in charge of change and they will almost inevitably contribute their energy and ideas. Even sceptics can be converted into advocates through this approach. Giving senior stakeholders authority over the direction and approach to change is an essential ingredient of success.

You cannot involve or empower all of the people all of the time, but the more you do to give people control the better. A successful change initiative cannot be introduced by the back door.

4.8   Senior stakeholders

It is essential when instigating large-scale change to have a senior or executive level individual who takes accountability for its success and drives activity. They provide guidance, spearhead communication, and manage other senior players within the organisation, ensuring that they are kept on-side and the initiative does not fall foul of boardroom politics.

Having the right senior sponsor(s) is critical. It is easy to get it wrong. For instance, there is a strong temptation for a chief executive or board of director to nominate the IT Director to sponsor a change that involves new IT systems or the Finance Director to sponsor cost saving initiatives, when in reality it is the Operations Director (or someone similar) who has responsibility for the people who will actually use the new IT system or who have to drive out cost efficiencies. Giving authority over change to the wrong person causes all sorts of issues, as people experience a disconnect between the project sponsor exhorting them to work differently and their "real" boss who they look to for leadership and who is apparently not involved in the change. In this type of situation, it is a major uphill battle to get people to adopt the change. Authority over change must be put in the hands of the right person or people i.e. those with authority over the people most affected by the change.

The success of any major initiative is dependent on the commitment of a range of people in senior positions, so it is worthwhile spending some time considering their specific need for control during change.

By their nature, senior leaders are unlikely to want to "ride in the back of the bus", especially when the change you are proposing affects their area of responsibility. One effective way of getting them involved and also giving them authority is to co-opt them on to some form of steering committee that provides oversight for the programme of change. An alternative, but somewhat less effective approach, is to consult with them about the change and to provide them with regular updates on progress. Yet another is to co-opt their direct reports on to the project team, so that they have people on the inside who they know and trust and who they can rely on to protect their interests and provide them with inside information on project progress.

How much control people need is dependent on the scale of the change and the level of trust in the organisation. A small change in an organisation where people trust one another to do the right thing requires some information and discussion and then people can be left to get on with it. For large changes, where there is a history of failed initiatives and a culture of silo working, a great deal of power-broking is required. In this case, getting consensus amongst the right people is a very important job which consumes a significant amount of time and energy. However, it is time well spent as without their genuine and active support you will almost inevitably fail.

4.9 The middle management black hole

A common complaint executives often have about change is that their managers have let them down. The directors have become convinced of the importance of a given initiative and communicated this to their managers, who then fail to motivate their teams to make it happen. The executives are frustrated that their enthusiasm for change appears to have been sucked into a "Middle Management Black Hole". Meanwhile, the middle managers feel like the meat in the sandwich, caught between gung-ho directors and staff members who are fearful of change.

Take the simple example of a Chief Executive who decides to introduce a quality and efficiency programme known as Lean Manufacturing. He and his fellow directors have a strong belief that this programme will create huge benefits for everyone in the organisation.

The Chief Executive, backed up by the Operations Director, launches the initiative to the middle management team, who raise a lot of questions and concerns about how it will work and fail to get as excited at the prospect of change as their bosses are.

The middle managers have not been party to the discussions leading up to the decision to introduce Lean Manufacturing and few of them have any experience of making it work. They also have little idea about what it will mean for them. They are now faced with the prospect of converting their teams to new ways of working which they don't really understand and which may threaten their positions as leaders in their own parts of the business. It would hardly be surprising if they became a blockage in the works.

Middle managers have a tough time during major change. They need to keep on delivering day-to-day results whilst at the same time preparing themselves and their teams for change. Their bosses may be exhorting them to communicate the benefits of change one minute and then interrogating them about why performance has slipped the next. Their teams may be asking them for answers about the change which they simply cannot answer, whilst they themselves may be full of doubt about a change over which they have had little or no influence. They may also feel out of their depth in dealing with the uncertainty and emotional strain affecting their teams. So it is easy to see why someone in this position might choose to focus on the day job rather than using up their valuable time on something as tricky as change. And that is how Middle Management Black Holes are created. They form an impenetrable layer between senior leaders and people on the ground blocking information flow and stifling the progress of change.

To avoid Middle Management Black Holes, managers must be engaged in the process of change and given control over it. In the example above, some of the managers should have been involved in the analysis that led to the decision to introduce Lean Manufacturing. They could have been given a crash course in Lean Manufacturing so that they felt in command of the subject and able to lead their teams with confidence. On top of that, they should have been equipped with the skills required to lead organisational change (described in this book). All of this would remove their motives for resisting change and help them take charge of it. With the middle managers willing and able to drive change you have every chance of turning your vision into a practical reality.

4.10 Trust

A recurring theme in this chapter and throughout this book is trust. Do managers trust their people to get on with things or do they feel the need to control them? People trust people like themselves to tell them the truth, warts and all, about change. If you don't work openly with people on change then trust is damaged. If people understand and trust efficiency methods, they will be far more supportive of efficiency initiatives.

Giving people control over change increases their level of trust in the change. In organisations where a high degree of trust already exists, open communications and an inclusive approach to change will be second nature. So change will be a collaborative process and trust will continue to increase in a virtuous circle. Where trust in an organisation is already low there will be a tendency to hoard information rather than share it and to tell people what to do rather than discuss proposals. These organisations are in a vicious circle of ever decreasing trust. If you are tasked with leading change in a low-trust environment you will need to work twice as hard to open up channels of communication and encourage consensus building so that people start to feel in control of change rather than being victims of it. The ultimate goal is to flip the organisation into a virtuous circle of increasing trust leading to an increasing ability to absorb change.

Summary

Lack of control over things that greatly affect us causes stress and anxiety. Having change 'done to us' by others leaves us feeling disrespected and powerless. All of this damages morale, increases opposition and reduces the chances of success.

Giving people control over their own destiny reduces fear and stress, increases support for change and improves the chances that it will be fully adopted by people. In addition, getting the people closest to the change involved leads to better designed change and more effective implementation.

Leaders should:

1. Give as many people as possible who are affected by the change involvement in or responsibility for designing and implementing it

2. Ensure all key stakeholder groups, including, where necessary, customers, suppliers or the general public are consulted about the change

3. Engage middle managers in defining and implementing change and ensure that they are well trained in how to lead change effectively

4. Communicate the change widely and promote dialogue

5. Bring some sceptics into the change team as they make powerful converts

6. Get negative issues out into the open so that they can be dealt with as problems rather than have them rumbling around unaddressed

7. Give people power over change by training them in the skills and attitudes they require to be successful in the changed world of work

8. Ensure that the right senior stakeholders have authority over the change.

Chapter 5

Connection

"A nail is driven out by another nail. Habit is overcome by habit."

Desiderius Erasmus (1466 – 1536)

5.1 Attachments

We all want to be liked, accepted, respected, appreciated, admired and loved by others. At the same time we like, accept, respect, appreciate, admire and love other people. It is the glue that holds societies, families and organisations together. Much of our happiness depends on it and much of our behaviour is driven by it.

We also develop strong bonds to a wide variety of ideas, objects and ways of doing things. Some of us connect strongly with our country, our city, our town or village. Some people identify so strongly with a football team that their happiness is dependent on its success or failure. For others, there is affiliation with a brand of clothing, a sports car, a flag, old steam engines, a rock band, a soap star or a favourite jacket that will never be thrown away despite having seen better days. Thus, from the first time we pick up a comfort blanket as a child we identify closely with and gain security from many things that are external to ourselves. These things are susceptible to change, and so when they do change we feel it deeply. Letting go of old relationships, old ideas, old things and old habits is one of the principal challenges of change.

Bonds of loyalty play a vital role in the armed forces. In the British Army, for instance, there is loyalty to Queen and Country, to one's regiment, to one's battalion and, perhaps most crucially, to your unit; the small group of people with whom you live and work day in and day out and who you may need to trust with your life one day.

At work, we connect with our team, our customers, our suppliers and other people we deal with. We connect with our company, our products, our role, our profession, our brand, the way we do things, our personal desk space and a host of other ideas and inanimate objects. Many engineers, for instance, are hugely fulfilled by the things they build, cartographers love map-making and coal miners are intensely proud of being miners despite (or perhaps because of) the great difficulties and dangers they face.

There is a big part of us that wants the long-standing connections we have to people and to things to remain unchanged. We are nostalgic about the way things used to be and mourn the loss of contact with old friends and loved ones. We even cling to harmful relationships and harmful things that we know are bad for us (like an unloving partner or too much fatty food). As the saying goes "Better the devil you know". Even in East Germany, where life under Communism was grim, there is now a growing nostalgia for the past. Those with a yearning for the old days can stay in hotels filled with old Eastern Bloc furniture and in certain shops you can once again buy Communist era food brands like "Socialist Mustard".

Our desire to connect with others means that we will often go to great lengths to match their behaviours. This conformity enables us to live and work together in harmony, but it can also serve to exclude people different from us whose ideas do not fit in with our norms. This peer pressure may well hold us back from daring to be different and embracing new ways that break the rules about 'the way things are done around here'. On the other hand, if handled correctly, peer pressure can create the groundswell of opinion required to tip the balance in favour of change and can lead to a new definition of the norms of behaviour.

One of the key skills you require to lead change successfully is the ability to loosen people's connection to old relationships, old ideas and old ways of doing things and create strong bonds to new relationships, new ideas and new ways of doing things.

5.2 People and things

When it comes to connection, some of us have a general preference for connecting with people whilst others prefer connecting with things. We sit at different points on the continuum illustrated in Figure 5.1. 'Things' can include ideas and activities (not centred on human relationships) as well as inanimate objects. Our preference for people or things plays a crucial role in how we work and often guides us in the type of work we choose to do. Holiday Resort reps, for instance, tend to love being surrounded by people, whereas many librarians have a love of books. Some people get their kicks from leading large teams, whilst others get them from creating novel computer programmes. Introverts enjoy connecting with their own thoughts and value opportunities for peace and quiet. For them, the introduction of an open-plan office may be far from welcome.

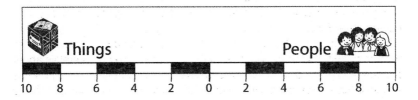

Figure 5.1 Connection Continuum

Organisational change will alter some of our connections with people and things. We may struggle to adjust to new relationships with colleagues, customers and suppliers. Equally, we can find it hard to give up old routines, old rituals and familiar ideas in the name of progress.

Take, for instance, the chargehand on a construction site who is promoted to foreman and has to manage a gang of men. If he wants to maintain the old relationships he had with the other chargehands, if he wants to remain their 'mate', he is going to struggle to lead the team, especially when it comes to dealing with issues of poor performance.

Chapter 2 introduced the idea that people's readiness to face uncertainty differs according to their personality and circumstances. Each of us, depending on who we are and the situation we find ourselves in, will tend towards a desire for *Stability* or *Exploration* as illustrated in Figure 2.3.

If we combine Stability Continuum, in Figure 2.3, with the Connection Continuum, in Figure 5.1, we end up with the Four Change Archetypes; Visionary, Researcher, Implementer and Carer, illustrated in Figure 5.2.

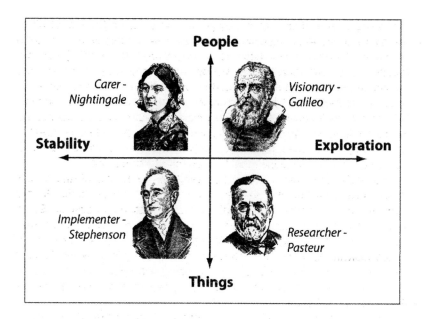

People

Carer -
Nightingale

Visionary -
Galileo

Stability

Exploration

Implementer -
Stephenson

Researcher -
Pasteur

Things

Figure 5.2 Four Change Archetypes

A Visionary is someone who is more attached to people than things and who prefers exploration to stability. They tend to be people who are looking to push the boundaries and to bring other people with them. They are entrepreneurs, generals, revolutionaries and trade union leaders. They may be people in your organisation who are not yet recognisable as leaders but who will emerge during times of change when they see an opportunity to do something new and to inspire others to come along for the ride.

In the famous science fiction television series Star Trek, the character of Captain James T Kirk typified the Visionary style. His stated mission was 'To boldly go where no man has gone before'. He acted on instinct, took great risks and inspired loyalty and admiration amongst his crew. First Officer Spock, the 'Researcher' in Figure 5.2, was Kirk's right hand man. Spock was also driven to seek out new planets and new civilisations, but his interest was born far more of intellectual curiosity. He worked with facts and figures and regarded human emotion (he was a Vulcan) as irrational and serving little useful purpose. Dr McCoy on the other hand, the 'Carer', was driven mainly by the desire to safeguard people's wellbeing or save their lives if they got into trouble. He frowned at Kirk's cavalier attitude to taking risks unless there was a humanitarian cause to be pursued – he was often heard to intone gravely "but Jim [Kirk] there are people *dying* out there". Like McCoy, Scotty the Chief Engineer, the 'Implementer', was not as interested in exploration as Kirk and Spock but much more motivated by tackling practical problems in the here and now. What worried him about the foolhardy exploits of Captain Kirk was not the danger to life and limb but how they might endanger his beloved spaceship the Starship Enterprise. Naturally, Scotty spent most of his waking hours closeted away in the engine room to keep the Starship going.

As individuals, our personalities tend to be a mix of these four archetypes. However, we do lean more towards one of them. All four archetypes are needed to bring about major change successfully. Some people must take the first bold steps and inspire support from others (the Visionaries), whilst others assess data and draw up models of how things could look in the future (the Researchers). Some will draw up detailed project plans and organise people to turn those plans into reality (the Implementers), whilst others will work out how people will be affected by the change and help them to make the journey (the Carers).

Where one or more archetypes are missing from a project team, things are liable to go wrong. For example, if you have a team of Researchers, they will spend endless days and weeks analysing the facts and trying to draw up the perfect plan (an impossible task) and will proceed very slowly to implementation. Meanwhile, they will have overlooked the need to involve people who are going to be affected by their new scheme as well as the need to persuade them that it is the right thing to do.

For instance, one group of academics who participated in a change leadership seminar I ran recognised that after their two universities had merged into one, many issues over the culture and values of the new institution remained unresolved as they had never been recognised as relevant. One lecturer described the combined university, which was located on two campuses as "mentally and physically divided" three years after the merger.

Similarly, a team comprised largely of Visionaries may never complete a successful change as they are prone to move rapidly from one great new idea to the next without following through to completion. A team of Carers may be so concerned with building consensus that they cannot react quickly enough to a need for change. Finally, a team of Implementers is so happy improving what is already in place that they may overlook the need to change altogether. Thus a balanced team is vital to the success of any change initiative.

5.3   Disconnection

From our earliest years, we have an overriding need to connect to other people and to feel appreciated, valued and respected. In the absence of this, many children will quickly resort to bad behaviour to grab the attention they need; a bad connection being preferable to no connection at all.

In society at large, problems arise when a group of people feel disconnected from the people around them. A shocking example of this took place in France in 2005 when a large number of second generation immigrants, mainly from North Africa, found themselves caught between an old country, where they had never lived, and a new one that treated them as outsiders. Lack of job opportunities and perceived prejudice against them eventually exploded into a wave of riots and destruction of property. Deep feelings of disconnection can unleash powerful reactions.

Whilst disaffected employees are unlikely to riot, the importance of keeping people connected is brought into sharp focus when a major change leads to a fundamental shift in the ethos of an organisation or people's place within it. If people no longer understand where they fit into an organisation they can become indifferent to its goals and lose motivation. This can happen, for instance, when a small organisation begins to grow and people start to feel that the organisation's leaders have become distant and the camaraderie of a close-knit team has been lost. Frequently, it occurs when one organisation is subsumed into another. If time and effort is not put into bringing people on board and helping them feel part of the family they will drift away mentally and eventually leave or, worse still, stay and just coast along.

5.4   Altering our connection to people and things

Ask any large organisation about its values and the chances are 'teamwork' will appear somewhere on the list. This is also reflected in the vast numbers of training and consulting companies offering team building activities ranging from psychometric testing to horse riding. All of this activity illustrates an appreciation by leaders of the value of collaborative teams and the destructive potential of dysfunctional ones.

If you have ever been part of a team that has operated under intense pressure in a tough environment and managed to succeed or just survive despite the odds, you will have experienced the strong connections that can form among work colleagues. Organisations invest millions of pounds each year promoting teamwork, yet they are surprised when people struggle to adjust as teams are broken up in a bid to improve organisational performance. There is no training course I know of that teaches good 'team demolition'.

When organisations change, teams, departments and even whole communities are broken up or re-located. There is a sense of loss and potential for a severe drop in morale unless time and effort are invested in building new connections. New teams need to be formed with new relationships and a common sense of purpose. This may seem obvious but it is not always well understood and can easily be overlooked in the commotion that often accompanies change. What is equally important and nearly always overlooked is how to lay to rest old relationships and old connections prior to moving onto the next new thing.

Also, we should not overlook the importance of relationships with external groups such as customers and suppliers. Changing these relationships can have a significant influence on people's attitudes to their job. For instance, a nurse may respond positively to an opportunity to take greater responsibility for patient care and to spend more time with patients. On the other hand, increasing her administrative duties may leave her feeling starved of contact with patients and diminish her drive and passion for the job.

A good example of the importance of external relationships is the case of a team of salesmen employed by a major UK beer brand who were asked to change the way they worked with their customers. For many years they visited pubs and took orders, negotiated prices, ran special offers and built relationships with the pub landlords. As competition stiffened and the market declined, they were asked to become more proactive in their approach to their customers and to tie landlords in more tightly to the brand. To do this, they needed to question the landlords about their business plans and help them out, for instance, with loans in exchange for preferential arrangements. The landlord could get a loan, for example, to build an extension and open up a restaurant area within the pub in exchange for stocking the brewer's wines.

The salesmen received thorough training in their new tasks and proved in role-playing exercises that they had mastered the required questioning and sales techniques. A new incentive system was created to encourage them to work more closely with landlords and by becoming their 'business partners'. But over the next six months nothing much changed. Sales continued to decline in line with the declining market.

Despite having the means and the motive to change why were the salesmen failing to make a difference? Investigation by the Human Resources Manager, who went out on sales calls with some of the salesmen, revealed that they were not even trying to become business partners. So were they just plain lazy?

At the request of HR, I spent a few days investigating why the salesmen seemed unwilling or unable to put what they had learnt into practice. Spending some time with them and digging deeper revealed that it was the change in relationship with their customers that sat at the root of the problem. As they themselves said, they had spent many years becoming the landlords' friend; some had even been invited to family weddings. Now they were expected to become their "banker", which just did not feel right.

The relationship between a salesman and a landlord had been a simple, friendly one based around selling as much beer as possible and making a good profit on all sides. Now much of this had to change and a new relationship forged. If old habits are hard to change, changing the nature of relationships is even harder, especially long-standing ones.

The salesmen needed a new outlook and a way of breaking the mould of their relationships. So they went back to the classroom to learn how to transform the way they related to their customers.

First, they took a step back and looked at the business environment as a whole and how the market had changed over recent years for the pub landlords and for the brand. They thought through the different strategies open to the company in the future and gained a better understanding of why they needed to create deeper business relationships with their customers. They also had open discussions to identify why it was so hard to break out of the current mode of working. By bringing all of the issues out into the open they were able to examine them objectively and work on solutions.

They worked out that they needed to move the relationship they had with their customers from uncritical friend to a more challenging friend who could help move their business forward. Between them they came up with a series of practical ways of breaking out of their old habit and relationships. For instance, they looked at key events in time such as the build up to Christmas and New Year which would provide ideal excuses for introducing new approaches to supporting their customers and help deliver some quick wins to build credibility. They role-played the precise conversations they would have with landlords in order to anticipate issues and gain confidence ahead of doing it for real.

Within weeks of the training it was clear from observing the salesmen in the field that they were shifting the base of the relationship they had with their customer, and within six months they were driving double-digit increases in year-on-year revenue from their customers.

The importance of relationships during change is also well illustrated by the experiences of people who have worked for a start-up organisation that subsequently experiences rapid growth. In the early days, there are few people in the organisation who encounter all sorts of difficulties as they struggle to get up and running. There is typically a feeling of a close-knit team that collectively rolls up it sleeves and gets on with doing whatever needs to be done. The most junior person is likely to work shoulder to shoulder with the Chief Executive. As the organisation succeeds and grows, people begin to lose the feeling of closeness they once had. An administrator in one such successful start-up company said to me, "Things just aren't like they were in the good old days. I remember when we used to work with Andy [the MD] every day. Now we hardly ever see him."

As an organisation expands, the feeling of being part of a pioneering group of people setting out on a great adventure is no longer tenable and needs to be replaced with something else. In many growing organisations people start to develop more of a connection to the purpose and ethos of the broader organisation than to a single leader. They also connect to the sub-division of the organisation in which they work, which takes on some of the characteristics of the original close-knit group. Some organisations believe in the 'Rule of 50' which says that once an organisation reaches 50 people, it is time to split it up into smaller components, maybe even separate companies. Organisations of this size are on a human scale and can operate efficiently and effectively without the need for sophisticated systems and processes. When people all know one another, personal relationships hold the organisation together rather than systems and structure charts.

Finally, where change means redundancy, trust takes a heavy knock and connection is of paramount concern. It is vital that leavers are seen to be treated fairly; otherwise those who remain with the organisation will feel that everyone has been let down and that the bond of trust between an organisation and its employees has been damaged irreparably. Connection to the organisation needs to be built up during these difficult times by re-establishing a common sense of purpose, setting new objectives and bringing people together. It is up to leaders to acknowledge difficulties, communicate a clear of vision of the future and to develop their teams.

5.5   Ceremony

Throughout human history, important occasions like birth, coming of age, marriage and death, as well as annual events like the summer solstice or harvest-time, have been distinguished through elaborate rituals.

Marriage is one such event that involves fundamental changes to the ways in which a group of people relate to one another. It is obviously an important occasion in the lives of the bride and groom, but it also affects a much wider population. The relationship between mother and daughter or mother and son change fundamentally. Two families and two sets of friends are brought together perhaps for the first time. All of this requires a good deal of adjustment. In many cultures, wedding celebrations can go on for many days and are steeped in ritual that guides people through an experience that they may only encounter once in their lifetime.

In recent decades, society has changed dramatically in the west, but it was not so long ago that marriage entailed a bride leaving her parent's home to join her husband's family; often a husband and family she barely knew. The marriage ceremony and celebrations with all of its rituals and traditions gave the bride a chance to adjust to her new husband and family and for both families to come together and cement new relationships. Even today, for Orthodox Jews. the wedding celebration is followed by several days of further celebration at the houses of family and friends. In this way, their integration into their new wider family can start to take shape over an extended period of time. Ceremony provides people with the means to loosen and undo old ties and to fashion new ones through a form of group therapy.

When two companies, employing hundreds or thousands of people, merge, a great deal of effort is given over to due diligence. Much time is devoted to poring over finances, integrating IT systems, telling the stock market about synergies ("A match made in heaven") and drawing up new structure charts. More often than not, there is little, if anything, in the way of a 'marriage ceremony'.

So once the lawyers, accountants, IT people and process engineers have performed their surgery, the patient wakes up wondering why they are in so much pain. After a while it may dawn on leaders that people change more slowly and in more complex ways than systems and processes.

5.6   Mergers and acquisitions

Undoubtedly, changing or breaking relationships at work can leave people feeling disconnected from their colleagues and their organisation, reducing their drive and ambition and making it tempting to leave. This is a particular danger when one organisation is merged with another or when one takes over the other.

Mergers or acquisitions present one of the biggest challenges to the way in which people connect to one another. Two organisations with differing approaches to working with customers, suppliers and colleagues are brought together as one. Unsurprisingly, the world of business is littered with failed marriages between seemingly compatible partners where the whole is meant to be greater than the sum of the parts. As one study published by accountants KPMG in 1999 revealed, 83% of all mergers and acquisitions fail to increase shareholder value[1].

There are many reasons why mergers and acquisitions fail, from boardroom battles to unrealistic predictions about the benefits of bringing the two organisations together. A common and acute problem is a failure to recognise and deal with the issue of connection. Little focus is given to helping people leave old relationships, ideas, practices, and symbols behind and take on the relationships, ideas, practices, symbols and ethos of the new organisation.

Take the example of a US bank (first mentioned in Chapter 3) with operations in the UK, let's call them First Asset Bank, which acquired a UK-based subsidiary of a European bank – let's call it DIF Fund Management – as part of its expansion in Europe [all the names in this example have been changed to ensure anonymity]. The integration of DIF with First Asset's UK operations was carefully planned. The lawyers and accountants did their work with no major

problems and once the deal was completed the parent company quickly got stuck into integrating UK and US IT systems and standardising business processes and organisation structures across the two companies.

DIF had been in business for over 100 years and, whilst it was by no means a dominant market player, it was highly profitable. Naturally, there was a strong sense of identity within the company, a good deal to be proud of and a very independent spirit to boot. Partly due to the confidential nature of merger negotiations, nothing was done to engage with UK employees ahead of the deal being finalised. Unfortunately, this was a trend that continued for quite some time after the take over.

Several months after the acquisition, there was a good deal of unhappiness amongst staff in the acquired company. In some locations, new divisions were formed comprising staff from First Asset (UK) and DIF. In these locations, where people from both organisations worked alongside one another, it still took quite some time before people felt like they were part of a single team. But in Belfast, the only representative of the parent company was the divisional MD, Jon Bryant, who found himself completely isolated. Even his leadership team struggled with, and to a large degree opposed, the changes set out by head office in Philadelphia.

Prior to being acquired by First Asset, DIF had been left pretty much to its own devices by its parent company in Europe (including keeping its name) which had bought it as part of a wider acquisition before selling it on once more two years later. Now, not only did DIF managers (who were now First Asset managers) have to report regularly to US head office, but sub-functions had to report to function heads in different locations around Europe in a matrix structure. The US sales approach seemed much more data-driven with Customer Relationship Management (CRM) IT systems for capturing every client interaction and distinct sales and marketing approaches by customer type. Previously at DIF, experience and gut feel had been used ahead of data analysis. There had been a strong feeling that good business relied on building trust backed up by a reliable brand name.

Because very little had been done to communicate with the DIF employees about what it meant to be part of the new organisation, people felt confused and resentful. They were also prone to assume the worst, believing, for instance, that all of their hard work in developing customer relationships and providing good service were now being disregarded in favour of a more rigid by-the-numbers approach.

5.7 Reconnecting

The issue at DIF was not simply one of communication. Where an organisation with its own history and culture is taken over, people need the opportunity to renew their sense of belonging and to adapt or transform their relationships with colleagues and customers (or else make an informed decision to leave). Whilst the First Asset's predicament was not unusual, their solution was as follows:

A new senior HR Manager, Chris Brown, became aware of the problem soon after her arrival at First Asset UK. She had lived through some tumultuous times at her previous employer, seeing a string of bosses come and go and having to help manage downsizing and re-structuring at a bewildering rate. She had joined First Asset because it had a great set of values about looking after its people as well as an unswerving dedication to its customers. It felt like a breath of fresh air after her last company as it was clear to her that these values were sincerely felt at every level of the business. Chris was therefore surprised and dismayed to find large pockets of unhappy (ex-DIF) people within the bank.

A big part of the problem was that the culture of the US company was so strong and so well understood by its staff, most of whom had only ever worked for First Asset, that it had not even occurred to them to explain it to the people in the newly acquired organisation. They had simply expected people to welcome with open arms the opportunity to work for such a great company.

Chris understood the issues instinctively, but felt like a lone voice and was not entirely sure of the remedy. She called up Claire Paten, an industrial psychologist well versed in organisational change, with whom she had worked at her previous company and together they began devising a programme to turn things around.

They started with the isolated business unit in Belfast where the problem was most acute and where even the leadership team was far from happy with the change. They knew that they had to begin at the top to stand any chance of success, so they spent some time meeting senior managers one-to-one and preparing a two-day off-site session with the MD, Jon Bryant, and his direct reports. The aim was to educate them about change and to help them overcome their own difficulties before going on to lead their teams into a new future.

The two-day event, held in Belfast, was led by Claire and Chris and opened with an indispensable technique known as the Timeline Method. This is a group activity that begins with the drawing up of a timeline illustrating the key events in the lifecycle of a change, usually on a large sheet of paper pinned to a wall (see Figure 5.3). These events can be internal to the organisation or external events that affect the organisation (such as legislation change or competitor activity). The timeline is then used to uncover how people responded to each event and to bring issues and emotions out into the open.

The Belfast leadership team set to work on the events leading up to and following on from the acquisition of DIF by First Asset. These included everything from being acquired by their previous parent company to the first time people heard about a possible take over by First Asset to the launch of a Customer Relationship Management (CRM) system.

For each major milestone, they identified assumptions they had made, expectations they had had and what had actually happened. They wrote these on pieces of coloured card and attached them to the timeline. For instance, when the new matrix organisation structure was announced they *assumed* that the functional heads based in centres around Europe would be their bosses and so their *expectation* was the people sitting in different geographic locations to them would be telling them what to do and autonomy would be lost. *What actually happened* was that the functional heads had more of an advisory and strategic role and they had been left very much to their own devices on a day-to-day basis and continued to report into their existing (ex-DIF) bosses. So there had been a good deal of angst at the time for no good reason.

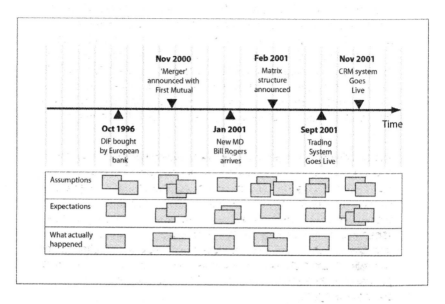

Figure 5.3 The DIF / First Asset (UK) Timeline

The timeline process does a number of things. Firstly, it gets the issues out in the open and distinguishes facts from assumptions and hearsay. Emotions can be expressed in a systematic way and put on the table for discussion rather than being kept bottled up inside and expressed only through general dissatisfaction or dysfunctional behaviour at work. Also, negative emotions can be dissipated by translating them into concrete problems for the group to solve together. Once out in the open, problems can seem diminished or be consigned to the past. This has a strong cathartic effect on people, allowing them to put issues behind them and move forward.

The timeline also allows people to gain a new perspective on their situation and the circumstances that brought it about. They can see how the organisation has responded to major external events and how internal actions have followed on from each other. People begin to v͡ ͡the current change as part of the ongoing evolution of their organisatio   ͡ as an anomaly to be rectified. It often becomes clear͡ discussions that without change the organisation will ͡ (such as the benefits of new technology) or fall foul of ͡ (such as loss of key personnel to competitors). Diss͡ status quo is an important counterbalance to peopl͡ keep things as they are and can help loosen ties with the past. The timeline method also begins to direct people's attention to the future and what it is they will need to do during the latest evolutionary phase to be successful.

Another useful process the Belfast leadership team at First Asset went through was to complete a Lose-Gain Grid. This simple grid was used during change to identify what people had lost, what they had kept and what they had gained (see figure 5.4). The Lose-Gain grid allowed them to distinguish things they supposed lost that had not actually been lost. Claire Paten gave people time to talk openly about what was being left behind and to formally put these things behind them. It is, of course, possible that this exercise leaves some people feeling that they have lost too much and so needs to be handled with care as these people may conclude that they wish to leave the organisation.

The leadership team were able to take comfort from what had been retained and to build on what had been gained. They came to appreciate that far from being a threat, the acquisition opened new doors to them. New systems and approaches imported from the US combined with their own skills and experience would enable them to be even more successful than before, and being part of a global organisation offered them new career opportunities. Perhaps more importantly, they found that the new systems and new structures did not mean jettisoning their approach of building long-term customer relationships. Far from it – in fact First Asset had built its reputation on just such an approach for over 80 years.

People	Lose	Keep	Gain
	• Some aspects of old client management approach • Previous MD	• Existing client relationships • Teams	• Better relationship management / client information
Things	**Lose**	**Keep**	**Gain**
	• UK identity • Brand name • IT system	• Existing roles • Many existing processes	• Career opportunities • Better IT systems • Bigger market presence

Figure 5.4   Things lost, kept and gained in the acquisition of DIF

Another powerful exercise involved Jon Bryant working with Chris Brown and a member of the leadership team to create at timeline for First Asset Bank as a whole, from its founding in Philadelphia at the end of the 19th Century to the present day. Jon spent time walking his team through the history of the company, describing critical events and explaining the company's values and how they manifested themselves in the way people worked together. He also spelt out a strong positive vision for the future of the organisation which he believed would continue to grow profitably, as it had done for many years, creating excellent career opportunities for its people.

By helping people engage with the change and by bringir ˙˙sues out into the open for discussion the leadership team be connect with the organisation, its values and its purp second day they had a better understanding of their r to change and had begun to transform their attitude⸍ had happened to them and how they should behav⸍

Claire Paten also worked with the team on a number of the elements of change covered in this book with the aim of better equipping them to lead their people along the journey of change that they themselves had just embarked upon. Their focus shifted to how they could engage the hearts and minds of the rest of their people using a similar process to the one they had just been through. Many of the senior managers were transformed from sceptics to enthusiasts – so much so, that when it came time to devise methods to engage their teams they were determined to do something remarkable. In particular, they had latched on to what Claire had told them about the role of ceremony in change and decided, amongst other things, to create an event that combined elements of a wake, a marriage and a New Year celebration. This would fulfil a strong desire to pay respect to the history and achievements of DIF and to celebrate the birth of a new and unique organisation. The whole would become truly greater than the sum of the parts.

Chris now found herself riding on a wave of enthusiasm. A team building event involving all Belfast employees was scheduled for a month after the leadership team event. The whole leadership team would be involved in designing and running the event to capitalise on their combined skills and to illustrate their commitment to the process.

On the first day of the event people were put into groups and each group took turns to go through different activities facilitated by members of the leadership team. One activity involved an enormous timeline pinned to a wall. People were invited to post up their thoughts (just as the leadership team had done previously) and to talk about how they had reacted to different important events. Another exercise involved completing and discussing a Lose-Gain Grid.

Other activities involved members of the leadership team explaining and discussing various contentious issues such as 'How we work with clients', 'How we are structured', 'Our values' and 'Our future strategy'. Everyone was invited to speak freely and to challenge what they saw. There was a lot of work carried out in groups to devise new ways of operating that brought together the best of the old organisation with all that First Asset had to offer.

There was a large poster on one wall entitled 'Things I will leave behind'. People were invited to write on the poster about old ways of working that would be left behind. Stacked below it were items that Chris and others had collected that symbolised the past. These included many signs, posters emblazoned with old company logos as well as diagrams and binders full of old process diagrams and guides to the old ways of working. Opposite to this was a First Asset poster entitled 'New things I will do' and on this people were encouraged to stick postcards addressed to themselves pledging one or two key things they would do to help bring about a new and more successful organisation.

In the afternoon and evening of the first day, there was a big celebration. There were comments and speeches from a wide range of people from the most junior administrator to Jon Bryant. People talked about the successes of the past, the difficulties of change and ideas for the future.

The poster entitled 'Things I will leave behind' and symbols of the past that had been gathered together were ceremonially sealed in a large container. Chris made a short speech before the container was carried shoulder-high out of the room amidst cheers and applause. All of this was followed by a large fireworks display. It was an exciting moment filled with great hope.

After that day there was a good degree of optimism within the organisation and people felt far more engaged in the future of the company. Chris made sure that it did not end there. She worked hard with the leadership team to keep up a steady flow of communication and activity to reinforce the messages from the day and to encourage people to gather behind a common cause.

The enthusiasm and feel good factor that was emanating from the UK was recognised in the US and Chris Brown soon found herself in Philadelphia presenting to the corporate Board. Within two years she moved out to the United States to head up Organisational Development which involved her supporting a range of major change projects across First Asset.

Summary

Old habits die hard. We develop strong attachments to ways of working and who we work with. Helping people let go of old connections and forge new ones is a critical element of leading successful change.

Leaders should:

1. Start by understanding which relationships, ideas, symbols and work routines will be affected by change.

2. Help people sort fact from assumptions and hearsay.

3. Help people discover why standing still would leave the organisation vulnerable to outside threats or result in valuable opportunities being missed.

4. Bring issues associated with change out into the open so that they can be addressed.

5. Allow people to acknowledge and regret the loss of old connections but also to put the past behind them using ceremony.

6. Help people forge new connections based on new approaches and a new sense of purpose.

7. Bring together a balanced team of Visionaries, Researchers, Carers and Implementers to deliver the change.

Chapter 6

Success

6.1 The role of success

We strive for success from our earliest days. It drives our childhood development from learning to crawl to throwing a ball to riding a bicycle. As we grow up, success becomes more complicated – winning at sport, passing exams, raising happy children, hitting production targets, getting promoted, developing our team or making customers happy. Deprive us of success and we become disillusioned and despondent.

Deprive an organisation of success and it can trigger a downward spiral as failure leads to loss of confidence, bad publicity and the loss of good people, leading to still worse performance. It then takes dynamic leadership, a renewed sense of purpose and a great deal of effort to turn the tide and to spin the organisation into a virtuous circle of improved performance and greater confidence which leads to growing success. Thus, a steady flow of success is vital to the health of both individuals and organisations.

Success may be its own reward, bringing with it personal satisfaction and increased self-esteem, but the effect is even more powerful when reinforced by external recognition. As any parent knows, children don't just want to succeed, they want to be seen to succeed. In fact, achieving a new goal, like learning to tie a shoelace, seems barely to count until a parent has witnessed it. Even as adults, the approval and appreciation of others remains a powerful and central motive for continuing to strive for success. As most people will testify, devoting a large amount of time, energy and emotion to achieving a tough goal at work can be hugely satisfying. However, if all of your efforts go unrecognised and are not even acknowledged with a simple 'thank you' it can be a very frustrating and demoralising experience. Well-considered and well-timed recognition of the effort put in by others is an essential part of good leadership.

The link between success and recognition is measurement. Some form of measurement is required to gauge success before it can be recognised, and it is often the measurement itself that guides behaviour, not the achievement of the desired outcome. It is now a cliché in business that 'What you measure is what you get'. For instance, measuring and rewarding achievement of sales targets will undoubtedly increase sales, at least in the short run. However, if sales volume is the only measure then some salespeople may cut corners and resort to hard selling tactics in a bid to beat targets and increase their bonus payments. In the long run, customers will be put off by pushy salesmen and will look elsewhere to more user-friendly suppliers. Thus, unless the incentive scheme recognises other factors, like customer satisfaction, it ends up producing quite the opposite effect to what was originally intended. Recognising success should be treated with care.

So what happens to success when a major change comes along? To use a familiar sporting analogy, the goalposts get moved. Not only that, but the rules of the game or even the game itself may change. Success becomes harder to understand, let alone achieve. At the very time when it is most needed to boost confidence and to sustain people through a period of uncertainty success can become elusive.

Success is the oxygen that allows new ideas and new methods to spring to life and bear fruit. If success is not nurtured and recognised then the 'teething problems' and early failures that typically accompany change will cause it to come unstuck and all your efforts to improve performance will go to waste.

6.2 The changing nature of success

As the world changes, so does our definition of success. In recent decades, Western society has changed dramatically. For instance, gender roles have become progressively less and less stereotyped. More women now work, many juggling this with motherhood or opting not to have families at all, something that was a rarity only a generation or two ago. At the same time, men's roles are shifting. For instance, it used to be that fatherhood was about a man providing for his family by going out to work to earn a living. Nowadays, it is increasingly to do with raising children and sharing the domestic burden (though the latter still appears to be a long way off). For husbands and fathers, income used to be a significant measure of success, but now it is not uncommon for mothers to be the main breadwinner in the family. As a result, both sexes are struggling to understand the new rules of the game let alone what it means to be successful. This struggle with uncertainty all adds to the stress and strain of modern life.

Similarly, human relationships at work have changed in what is often referred to as the 'feminisation' of the workplace. Leaders are expected to nurture and support the development of their people, to communicate openly, help people to learn from their mistakes and praise their successes. There is a good deal more emphasis on Emotional Intelligence – being able to empathise with people and respond appropriately to their different needs. Seniority in the hierarchy is no longer a guarantee of respect. Leaders must earn people's respect through how they behave.

Dramatic shifts in the definition of success challenge organisations as well as individuals. Fears about global warming, for instance, have caused many enterprises to re-think their responsibilities to the rest of society. A few years ago, nobody talked about carbon footprints. Now it has become a fundamental part of corporate and government strategy. Journalists now quiz airline executives as much about the effects of their aircraft on global warming as they do about airfares or customer service.

As the rules change, it is hard to know just what is expected of us and whether it will be different again next year. Such uncertainty can undermine our confidence and our ability to make decisions based on shifting criteria.

In sport, we wouldn't dream of changing the rules of the game without ensuring that players, referees and fans were all clear about what was going on and were able to play their part in ensuring a smooth transition. The same should be true in our own organisation. If, for instance, you wish to instil a culture of good customer service or a risk-taking 'entrepreneurial' culture there is a big job of work to be done to spell out the new rules of the game, the new ethos and what is expected of people on a day-to-day basis. There needs to be clarity amongst employees, customer, suppliers and shareholders about what now constitutes success. Support (including training) should be provided to equip people to achieve new goals. All of this must be cemented into place through recognition and reinforcement by leaders.

6.3 Incompetence and failure

Wholesale organisational change can mean that our experience becomes less relevant and our skills outdated. We may need to go back to school, learn new skills and adapt to a new environment. This is a daunting prospect, which can lead to feelings of incompetence and fear of failure resulting in a loss of confidence and a drop in performance.

To compound the fear of failure there is every chance of actual failure as people get to grips with new systems, new expectations and new ways of doing things. People are obliged to keep faith in approaches which they perhaps mistrusted in the first place, despite getting worse results than before. Cue the cynics who have been biding their time in the wings. Their prophecies of doom now appear to have come true. Their sniping at "another crazed initiative handed down by head office" will feed off the real difficulties that people experience as they transition to the new reality and can encourage some not to persevere with the change.

As we saw in Chapter 2, change is often accompanied by a drop in performance (see Fig. 2.2). As people transition to new ways of working, their performance can be characterised typically by Performance Curve A or Curve B illustrated in Figure 6.1.

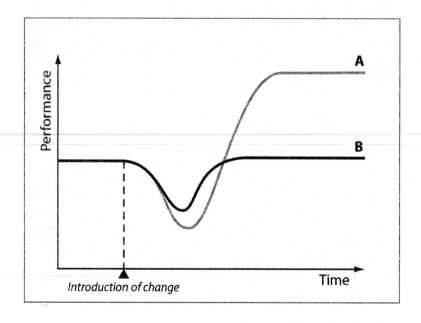

Figure 6.1 *Performance Curve A and Curve B. Curve A is experienced by people who persevere with change, Curve B by people who give up on change when their performance drops.*

Anyone who has been coached in sport can easily appreciate these two responses to change. Take, for instance, sports like golf or tennis where getting your grip right on the club or racquet is all important. What is the first thing that happens when you go for lessons in the hope of improving? The coach takes one look at your grip and informs you that it needs to change if you want to take a step up to the next level of performance. So you try out the new grip during the next round or two of golf or the next few tennis matches with your friends and you follow Performance Curve A or Curve B.

In Curve A you try out the new grip and find your performance drops as you struggle to adjust to it. You lose at golf or drop some sets at tennis and curse your instructor. But there is the odd moment of joy as you hit a beautiful shot. This, combined with your faith in your instructor, time spent on the practicing your shots and the strength of your desire to improve, is enough to convince you that perseverance will pay off. After several more rounds of golf or tennis matches you are performing on a new plane and all the effort and frustration has been worthwhile.

On the other hand, in Curve B you lose a game of tennis to someone you habitually beat or you spend an afternoon searching for your golf balls in the bushes and you simply revert back to your tried and trusted grip. Your play will improve gradually over time, but you will never achieve a quantum leap in performance. The money for the lessons has been wasted.

Curves A and B are also what people experience at work.

Take the example of the high street retailer that was losing out to competitors it had once dominated. The new CEO decided, unsurprisingly, that one of the main routes to regaining its pre-eminent position was to deliver exceptional customer service. Part of the plan for doing this was to get the sales assistants in their stores to engage more actively with customers. This included assisting women customers by suggesting other clothes or accessories to go with what they were already trying on. By helping the customer create an outfit rather than simply finding a skirt in the right size, the sales assistants would improve service to the customer and increase sales.

But people who have operated in an unchanging environment for a number of years are likely to be worried by the thought of approaching work in a different way. The sales assistants who had

been happy helping customers find what they wanted were alarmed by the prospect of suggesting a blouse to match a skirt or a handbag to complete an outfit. How should she (or he) start the conversation? What if the customer did not want to be helped? What if she made a fool of herself? Some started to wonder if they had the wherewithal to do their job. There was every chance that they would follow Curve B, which would lead the whole organisation along Curve B.

The introduction of new information technology also typifies this point.

Back in the early 1990s, I worked with an accounts department in a government agency on the automation of their general ledger processes which were still largely paper-based.

The department head was a good manager, who had been in the Civil Service for over 30 years. She got on well with her staff and was very helpful in ensuring that the project stayed on track. It was only when we got into the classroom that I realised how difficult things were going to be for her.

In the training course that preceded the roll out of the new IT system, everyone had their own computer terminal on which they were expected to carry out a series of case study exercises. A number of people, especially the younger ones, picked things up quickly and stormed through the exercises, while others stared at the keyboard struggling to find the right key to press. Some of the participants, who had managed to enter the data required, then proceeded to hover endlessly over the 'Enter' key as if it were the nuclear button.

As for their boss, tears welled up in her eyes as she struggled to get to grips with the new system as the junior members of her team raced ahead. At a time when she most needed the self-confidence to lead her team into the new world of technology, she was questioning her own competence.

Fortunately for all of us, she worked hard to master the new technology, taking time after the training sessions to ask questions and take tips from us on how to get the most from the system.

What is more, she remained positive about the change in front of her team. However, had she been a less open-minded individual she might have made life extremely difficult for us and discouraged her team from taking the new system seriously, finding excuses not to drive the project forward. Perhaps more importantly, once the system was up and running and the project team disbanded, it would have been easy for her not to make full use of the system. She might even have run the old system in parallel with it (something I witnessed in other organisations).

Returning to the retail store sales assistant, we can imagine how she felt the first time she suggested a blouse to go with a skirt that the customer had asked to try on. She may have felt awkward and embarrassed. She may have worried that she had made a hash of it even when the customer followed her suggestion. The easiest course of action for her at this point would have been to retreat back to the comfort of her old way of working, giving customers only what they asked for and standing guard at the changing room door. Fear of failure is often much stronger than the desire to achieve greater success.

Performance Curve B explains the mystery of the missing performance improvement that so often baffles leaders following a major transformation programme.

6.4 Leadership and success

The simple and familiar process illustrated in Figure 6.2 describes how leaders should measure, recognise and nurture success at work. It begins with setting expectations and goals (defining success) and then communicating them to members of the team. Once people are clear about what is expected of them they can then take action at work. The results of people's efforts can then be gauged using measurement systems that vary from straightforward observation of behaviour (by a manager) to a performance appraisal system measuring a range of factors from on-time delivery to customer satisfaction. People are then recognised for their successes or coached to improve where performance falls short of expectations.

This success process is central to managing performance and in most organisations a good deal of time and effort goes into developing incentive schemes, setting production targets or creating performance measurement systems. Get your measurements wrong and you can create all sorts of perverse incentives which prove counterproductive. For example, incentivising a call centre agent to keep calls as short as possible can increase productivity but reduce customer satisfaction as agents try to end conversations without resolving problems properly. Play around with people's targets or ignore their achievements and you quickly run into trouble. Similarly, when change comes along the success process can be thrown off balance unless every link in the chain is attended to effectively.

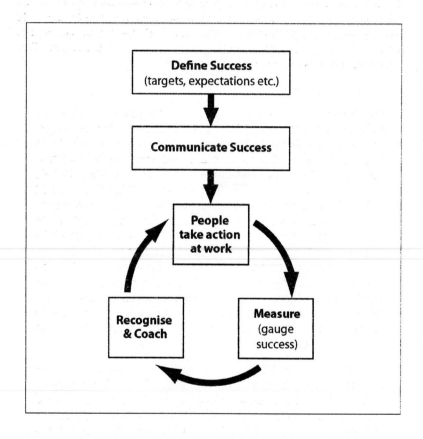

Figure 6.2 Success Process

6.5 Define success

The first link in the chain is the definition of success. In adjusting successfully to change, people need the answers to questions such as "What new activities will I need to carry out and how should I do them?", "How do I need to work with other people?" and "What is the vision and rationale for change?"

Generally speaking, it is easy to explain what you want from people in terms of new tasks and responsibilities. One can illustrate what's required using process flow diagrams, organisation structure charts and role descriptions. Where organisations often fall short is in the trickier area of explaining changes in vision, philosophy and expected behaviours. This can lead to unexpected and undesired results.

Take the example of a major manufacturer in the UK in the 1980s that was switching from UK-based to overseas (and less expensive) component suppliers. For the first time, they now had to deal with factories based on the other side of the world whilst remaining quick and efficient in bringing new products to market. To help them achieve this they installed a Computer Aided Design (CAD) system. Their designers were asked to switch from manual designs on paper, which worked well enough with local suppliers, to electronic designs which could be emailed to the other side of the world in a matter of moments. In addition, they needed to become more disciplined about making their designs more detailed and correct in the early stages of design rather than sending through imprecise specifications and then correcting them once sample components were provided by suppliers. Dealing with suppliers on the other side of the world meant getting things right first time to minimise time to market and to keep costs down.

The designers were duly trained on the CAD system and became competent pretty rapidly. All was sunny in the garden. Designers were able to pass their designs back and forth between the UK and various other countries based mainly in the Far East. The company had invested wisely and had taken a leap forward in speed and efficiency as well as reducing their cost base. Or had they?

Four months later, things did not seem to be moving much faster than before. The overseas suppliers knew why but they would not say anything for fear of rocking the boat and losing a major customer. However, at a supplier conference they did admit in private that there was little sign that the CAD system was being used. Imprecise designs were still being sent through by fax. So the investment in CAD was going to waste and the process of change had failed on a number of levels. How had this happened?

The answer to this question lay in a number of areas. First off, the CAD system implementation had been a major project. As with many large systems projects, it ran into technical difficulties and came under pressure to deliver to a tight deadline. When delivery became the focus of the project, attention was diverted away from the end users. As a result, training became more of an afterthought and what was put together was a highly functional view of what people needed to do, largely overlooking why they needed to do it. In particular, it ignored the important change in ethos to more of a partnership approach between the UK manufacturer and its suppliers. The designers now had greater responsibility for minimising the time it took to bring new products to market. In particular, they needed to help component suppliers minimise the lead time from receiving a design to manufacturing a component.

Designers had become used to suppliers who were at their beck and call. They could afford to continually adjust their designs and suppliers would dutifully produce new samples until the designers were satisfied. This was manageable with suppliers based in the UK though it added a good deal of hidden cost to the process, but now that they were working over long distances designers needed to adjust their own approach. The importance of this new partnership approach was not nailed in the training and commitment to change was not obtained from designers. Nor was this new behaviour followed up and reinforced by department heads after implementation, as performance management was weak within the organisation. As a result, designers reverted back to the tried and trusted method of trial and error, whilst the CAD system was largely ignored and product lead times got longer not shorter.

6.6   Communicate success

Once you are clear about what is to be expected of people as a result of change you then have the challenge of communicating all of its facets. This requires a sustained communication campaign (see Chapter 2) using all channels at your disposal such as presentations, emails and internal newsletters.

But if change requires new attitudes, behaviours and skills, then the cornerstone of communication is some form of training. Training offers a rare opportunity to address issues of ethos, attitude and behaviour as well as the acquisition of new skills in detail away from the distractions of day-to-day work.

In the case of CAD training for the manufacturing designers, the opportunity to instil a new ethos of partnership with suppliers was missed the first time round and had to be revisited several months later when it became clear that the design process had become slow and costly despite the investment in new technology.

Returning to our retail store sales assistants, practical training, including role-playing exercises, was crucial in avoiding Performance Curve B. They were given the opportunity to try out new methods of dealing with customers in an environment where failure was acceptable. This was an important step in adjusting to new working practices allowing them to begin to climb the learning curve before returning to work. As a result, sales assistants were far more confident about trying out the new approach and supporting each other as they did so.

6.7   Measure success

Whilst changes in behaviour begin with communication and training, it is through measurement, recognition and coaching that they are embedded.

The first task is to align measures, such as targets, to new objectives and new ways of working. Naturally enough, people will adjust their behaviours in line with new targets and measures, especially if they are linked to pay. For instance, telling buyers to build long term, mutually beneficial partnerships with suppliers is of no use if their bonuses relate solely to the sales margin they deliver. However, there are other issues to overcome.

As we have seen, people's performance will generally drop following a change and some may choose to follow Curve B. Output measures are generally a slow way of spotting problems. As with our manufacturing designers it may be weeks or months down the line before you detect that things have got worse rather than better, by which time it may be too late to fix them. Even then, you might not be sure if the downturn is simply due to teething problems as people adjust to new ways of doing things. Whatever the case may be, you will have lost out on revenue and you will need to invest more time and money in turning the situation around.

Meanwhile, your project will have lost credibility in the business and may have been fatally damaged.

What is needed is a focus on *behaviours* ahead of results. If you can get people to adopt the correct behaviours then results will follow. If things still don't improve then you know that there is a flaw in the initiative rather than a problem with how your people have put it into action.

In the case of the retail sales assistants, they needed to be consistently engaging with their customers in a new way. Measuring sales at the end of the week won't tell you if the sales assistants are offering suggestions to customers on which tops will go with the skirts they are buying. This can only be done through observation by peers, team leaders and managers. This requires managers who are skilled and motivated to manage performance and/or a culture which encourages peer-to-peer feedback as a means of development.

6.8 Recognise and coach success

Being recognised for what you do is particularly important during periods of change when self-esteem and confidence may be lower than usual and even a simple 'well done' can go a long way. You should pounce on every opportunity to publicise successes and encourage people to invest their time and energy in climbing Performance Curve A.

What often happens when people are trained in new skills and behaviours is that it is only when people get back to work that they fully appreciate the difference between what they have learnt and what happens in practice. The customer who had been so easy to negotiate with in the role-play may have a novel set of issues or, worse still, they may not even return your calls. This sort of experience can lead people to question the value of the training and tempt them to slip back into the old ways. It is therefore vitally important that leaders coach and support people effectively once they have returned to work. Following the measure and coach loop illustrated in Figure 6.2, they can encourage the right behaviours and support those who are struggling to succeed.

Another important element of recognition is the creation of heroes. Find some people who have made a successful transition to new ways of working and make sure that everyone knows about what a great job they are doing. Where a designer has used the new CAD system to bring a product to market in double quick time, get their director to come and congratulate them in person. For the sales assistant who has managed, despite early difficulties, to find her own way of engaging better with customers and delivering increased sales get a senior manager to sing her praises at a team meeting.

Understanding what it takes to be a hero is a powerful indicator to people of what is expected of them, so you must take care not to promote the wrong heroes. For instance, a major pharmaceutical company was on a mission to improve work-life balance amongst its sales teams. Whilst HR was making good headway in shifting people away from a mindset of working all hours, the CEO gave a video update to the organisation in which he picked someone out for special praise because they had just worked over the weekend to meet a proposal deadline. This may have been necessary and commendable but should not have been promoted and encouraged so as to be seen to exemplify the company ethos. As you can imagine, the HR Director just hung her head in despair at the sight of this.

6.9 Bite-sized successes

A useful technique for ensuring that morale is boosted on regular basis following change is to create a steady flow of success through short-term targets and milestones. Elite athletes will tell you that rather than setting their sights on a distant Olympic Games or World Championships, they will set themselves a series of graduated targets, like winning certain races or achieving particular finish times, in a steady build up to a major championship. In work, the same principle applies. When, for instance, a project team has a distant deadline or target to meet, a good project leader will create bite-sized successes that can be celebrated along the way as people find it far easier to remain focused on a short-term goal and are motivated by short-term success. As a result, people apply effort at a steady rate rather than working like crazy once the final deadline is in sight and perhaps missing the target altogether. By creating bite-sized successes, leaders can ensure that people remain positive about change and give it the time and space it needs to take root.

Finally, leaders need to be role models for the new behaviours if they are going to bring their people with them. It is no good if a store manager preaches better engagement with customers if they spend most of the day in a back office and rather than getting out onto the shop floor and showing people how it is done. Change begins at the top.

Summary

Following change, people can be fearful of failure, tempting them to backtrack out of changing the way they work. If people have confidence in their future success ahead of change and success is carefully nurtured following change, then people are far more likely to adopt new practices and make a step change improvement in their performance.

Leaders should:

1. Create and communicate a new definition of success, including what is expected of people, how they will achieve it and why they need to do it.

2. Align measurement systems to the new organisational objectives.

3. Provide thorough, practical training that emphasises the new definition of success.

4. Coach and support people as they get to grips with new ideas and ways of working.

5. Focus first on getting people to put the right behaviours into practice before becoming too concerned with results.

6. Act as role models for new skills and behaviours.

7. Train other leaders to appreciate Performance Curve A and Curve B and how to deal with them

8. Create heroes out of people who make a breakthrough in performance as a result of the change.

9. Take every opportunity to praise and reward people for practicing the right behaviours and to celebrate early successes.

10. Actively plan and manage the flow of success following a change through short-term goals that can be publicly celebrated.

SECTION 2

Implementing Change

Section 2 examines how to promote change within an organisation and the practicalities of implementing it.

Chapter 7

Creating a Tipping Point

7.1 The thrill of the new

On 24 January 1984, during a break in the final of the US Super Bowl, a TV advert was shown for the first time in the USA. Based on a theme from George Orwell's *1984*, it featured scores of grey faced, shaven-headed men dressed in grey, heads bowed, trudging mindlessly up and down enormous grey concrete staircases under the glare of a Big Brother figure bellowing out orders from a giant black and white television. Everything in the scene was desolate, dull and grey. Suddenly, an attractive, young, athletic woman dressed in brightly coloured running shorts and vest came sprinting in wielding a sledgehammer. She swung the sledgehammer round and hurled it at the giant screen. The screen exploded on impact letting off a huge shower of sparks. It was the legendary launch of the Apple Mac computer. The implication was that Big Brother, a.k.a. IBM, was about to be swept aside. A bright, new, exciting future awaited us all.

Not one word was spoken in the advert and the Apple logo appeared only right at the end. The advert was shown just once in the US. Nevertheless, the furore it generated was so intense that it received massive coverage in the media for a long time to follow. It is still regarded by many to be the greatest advert ever. Apple Macs flew off the shelves.

The prospect of change was enthralling. The 'early adopters' got the message straight away and bought out all the stocks. Millions of others followed in their wake.

Obviously, hype without substance quickly fades. But Steve Jobs, the founder of Apple, had a deep understanding of the future of personal computing and a product that was built on that understanding. As another less well known Apple advert put it, "If computers are so smart, why don't we teach them about people instead of teaching people about computers."

Looking at the example of Apple might make you wish that the changes you would like to introduce at work were as exciting as the launch of a revolutionary new computer. But in point of fact there were plenty of very good reasons for sticking with IBM. After all, they were the market leaders. They were highly reliable and most available software was written for use on IBM computers. Why would anyone want to switch from tried and trusted IBM who invented the PC? Anyway, was the Apple Mac really so different?

There is a part of us all that it attracted to the new. Why else would well known brands keep offering us 'All New!' versions of everything from cars to washing powders? All change has some level of thrill or intrigue. The job of a leader is to tap into this emotion and use it to tip the balance of opinion in favour of change.

7.2   The paradox of change

The story of the human race is one of continuous development, change and sometimes revolution. We are curious creatures who like to explore the unknown and are thrilled by the new. If you are in any doubt about this, try taking a child to the circus for the first time.

At the same time, we often greet new things with suspicion and fear, and can struggle to adapt to the changes taking place around us. We ask, "If it ain't broke, why fix it?" We like the comfort of the familiar; we like traditions that give us a sense of continuity and timelessness. This is the paradox of change. It is at once thrilling and scary, attractive and repulsive, vital and to be avoided.

Doing the same things day in day out eventually becomes dull and stultifying. It wears away people's sense of purpose and leads them to 'leave their brains behind' when they set off for work. We need the stimulation of new challenges to stay interested and engaged. Otherwise, we simply reserve all of our enthusiasm and creativity for our time away from work.

Think about the first day of a new job. Are you fearful that you may not be up to it or excited at the prospect of a new adventure? Most likely both to varying degrees, depending on a whole range of circumstances, such as your own appetite for change or the way you are brought on board by your new employer. Whatever the case, there are two opposing forces driving your response to the situation. Do we want the bright and exciting Apple Mac or the tried and trusted IBM PC? Do we want variety or do we want certainty?

7.3   The diffusion of innovations

Organisational change offers a chance to learn and grow. It is challenging and stimulating, and provides new experiences and the prospect of better ways of working. For those who sit at the 'Exploration' end of the Stability-Exploration Continuum (see Chapter 2) change is to be welcomed. For these 'Visionaries' and 'Researchers', the thrill of the new is a key motivator and drives them to select organisations and roles that offer them opportunities to explore new ideas and to break new ground. So don't be surprised when you set out your vision for change if a certain proportion of people are immediately excited by it and keen to contribute to its success. These individuals will be crucial in helping you get things rolling. Later on, as the change gains momentum, you will also need 'Implementers' to create detailed plans and to take action, and 'Carers' to help ensure people are looked after along the journey.

In 1962, Everett Rogers published a book called *Diffusion of Innovations*[1] which analysed how innovations caught on. Famously, he showed that adopters of any innovation or idea can be categorized as Innovators (2.5%), Early Adopters (13.5%), Early Majority (34%), Late Majority (34%) and Laggards (16%), based on a Bell Curve mathematic division (see Figure 7.1). Each adopter's willingness and ability to adopt an innovation depends on their awareness, interest, evaluation, trial, and adoption. People can fall into different categories for different innovations; a farmer might be an early adopter of hybrid corn, but a late majority adopter of MP3 players.

Rogers's research found that typically, **Innovators** are adventurous, use multiple information sources, and have a greater propensity to take risk. **Early Adopters** are often social leaders and popular. Members of the **Early Majority** tend to be deliberate in their thinking and have many informal social contacts, whilst members of the **Late Majority** tend to be sceptical, and traditional. He found that **Laggards** relied on friends and neighbours as their main information source and were highly averse to taking risks.

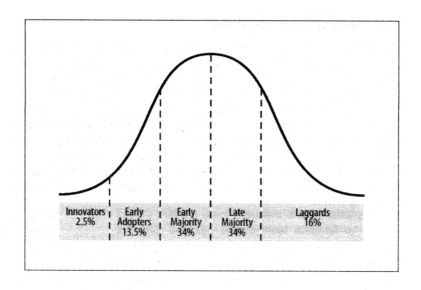

Figure 7.1 Readiness to adopt new products, from Everett Rogers 'Diffusion of Innovations', 1962

Rogers also proposed a five-stage model for the diffusion of innovation. It begins with the **Knowledge Stage**, where people learn about the existence and function of the innovation, the **Persuasion Stage** in which people become convinced of the value of the innovation and then the **Decision Stage** when people choose to commit to adopt the innovation. After that, comes the **Implementation Stage** as people put the innovation into use and finally the **Confirmation Stage** as the innovation is ultimately accepted (or rejected).

Rogers' findings have important implications for the uptake of change within organisations. Enthusiasm for any innovation will vary across the population of people it affects depending on people's natural disposition to change, as well as their feelings about what they and others stand to gain or lose ar   esult of the change.

7.4   Building momentum

The fashion industry is a perfect example of the diffusion of innovations repeatedly put into practice. The Innovators in this case are the fashion designers (who are themselves influenced by other Innovators from the world of art, dance or music). The Early Adopters are the fashion journalists and the celebrities that need to be seen in the newspapers and gossip magazines wearing the latest gear. Designers from mainstream retailers then take catwalk fashion and adapt it to the needs of the high street making it available to a wider population of consumers. The Early Majority are those people who go out and buy the latest fashions on the high street and the Late Majority and Laggards follow sometime after – or maybe never.

In the case of the internet, one of the greatest innovations of all time, the instigators where computer scientists in universities (the Innovators), who developed a system for communicating and sharing information amongst themselves. Then e-mail started to catch on as a means of general communication in places like Silicon Valley in California, where there was a large population of Early Adopters of technology, and eventually it moved into businesses and across the world reaching every corner of the globe.

Everett Rogers observed that Early Adopters tend to be social leaders and that the Early Majority tend to have many informal social contacts. This means that they will naturally have a disproportionate influence on the take-up of change by others. Some are trusted and experienced people whose opinion carries weight within the organisation, while others are 'natural networkers', people with extensive contacts throughout the organisation, who spend a good deal of their time seeking out the latest information and then disseminating it across the organisation.

When you are tasked with leading a major change you should seek out the Innovators and Early Adopters as they will be key allies in spreading change. They can easily be identified as they are not merely interested in change but have a passion for making it happen, often born of a real dislike of the status quo or a strong inner desire to improve things that need improving. They are the enthusiasts who enjoy trying out new ideas and can be relied on to run with new approaches despite uncertainties. They will infect others with their enthusiasm. You should seek out people who are widely respected and/or natural networkers, as they will play a crucial role in spreading messages about the change and can quickly tap into how people are responding to it, providing you with invaluable information about the take up of the change.

Many organisations select 'Change Champions' to spearhead new initiatives and deliver early benefits which give others the confidence to follow. They also act as role models, injecting enthusiasm for the change and later exemplifying the behaviours required for the change to succeed. This is invaluable in building up momentum for change, but has the potential danger that these self-selecting optimists with a natural interest in pursuing new approaches may not necessarily be trusted by others to be impartial. That is why it is good to co-opt a few people who are part of the Early Majority or Late Majority. They will be more trusted by others to present a balanced view of the pros and cons of a proposed change. You may even want to recruit some out-and-out sceptics and involve them in designing and implementing the change. This has its obvious risks but if you can convert them, then you neutralise their negative influence and they often become the strongest advocates for change.

Some enthusiasts are born and others are created. By experiencing a successful change in one part of the organisation, people who start out sceptical can become evangelists for change for the rest of the organisation.

In the case of Jamie's School Dinners, covered in Chapter 4, Jamie's greatest ally was Nora, the head cook at the first school he worked with. She had been highly sceptical to begin with, but over time and through experience she became a great advocate. Whilst she was not a natural Innovator, she became an enthusiast by finding out first hand how such a tricky project could be made to work. So when it came to talking to a much wider population of head cooks, she spoke their language and understood their concerns. She was living proof that it could be done and so had far more credibility than Jamie Oliver, who nevertheless injected passion and contagious enthusiasm into the process of converting others. This is an excellent illustration of how key individuals can have a significant role to play in galvanising wide-ranging support for change.

When you have the opportunity to roll out your change across different parts of the organisation over time, it is extremely helpful to co-opt people like Nora into your team and use them as ambassadors for change in other parts of the organisation which have yet to experience it.

As with the fashion industry, you want your novel ideas to become mainstream ones. Once you have your Early Adopters on board you need to coax the Early Majority using many of the techniques described in this book. You need to communicate continuously about the purpose and benefits of the change. You need to get people involved in designing and implementing change. You need to help people through the difficulties of letting go of old ways of doing things. You need to ensure that people are coached and supported and that you nurture and celebrate early successes. You also need peer pressure.

7.5 Tipping the balance

Human beings are social animals with a drive to conform to norms of behaviour, commonly known as peer pressure. It is peer pressure that persuades some of us to dress in certain ways and to behave in ways that are similar to or acceptable to our peers. This drive is well understood by the many organisations that are dedicated to helping people change their behaviour such as weight loss clubs, gym clubs and smoking cessation groups.

It is well known in the gym industry that people who visit the gym with an 'exercise buddy' are far more likely to stick with an exercise regime than those who exercise alone. An exercise buddy can provide encouragement and companionship, but more importantly we don't want to let them down by not showing up or to let ourselves down by not keeping up with them.

Weight loss clubs provide a similar story. Members can make common cause with other people and share their experiences, so they don't feel alone in their fight to stay away from the fridge late at night. But above all, there is the peer pressure of standing on the scales each week and being answerable to the group for our failings or applauded for our triumphs. People *can* lose weight on their own. They can weigh themselves at home and they can download diet information and meal plans from the Internet; they can buy low calorie foods in every supermarket and read about dieting in a thousand magazines and books. Yet a two year research study published in the *Journal of the American Medical Association* in April 2003[2] indicates that people who attended weekly weight loss club meetings fared much better than similar people who managed their own weight loss (in spite of the fact that these people were given two counselling sessions with a nutritionist and copious self-help resources). In fact, those on the structured club programme lost on average three times as much weight as their counterparts. So there must be something in it. It may be that weekly advice on diet and exercise provides a stimulus to stick to the regime. It may even be the thought of wasting the membership fee that spurs people on. But it is peer pressure that stands out as the major difference between joining a club and going it alone.

When a change has started to build momentum through Innovators and Early Adopters then it is up to the Early Majority to respond. The Early Majority are typically interested in new ideas and will be influenced by the Early Adopters whilst remaining more sceptical. They are likely to wait and see how the Early Adopters fare before dipping their toes in the water. If and when members of the Early Majority do start to come on board other members of the Early Majority (and Late Majority) will be encouraged to take the plunge, triggering a domino effect, fuelled by peer pressure, which will ultimately tip the balance in favour of change. It is therefore important when leading a change to intensify the pressure by publicising the early successes of people who apply the new practices at work.

You cannot convince all of the people all of the time. Early Adopters can become faint-hearted when faced with the trials and tribulation of making change happen in practice, and some sceptics will not be won over until the benefits become indisputable, perhaps months or even years after the fact. So an unremitting campaign is required using all of the 5 Forces of Change and spearheaded by a team of enthusiasts to build up a critical mass of people who can tip the balance in favour of change.

Finally, it is worth bearing in mind the value of branding your change initiative in building support, as we saw in Chapter 3. Branding elevates your initiative from the status of a project to something that embodies new ways of behaving and a new mindset. As with Plan A from M&S, a brand provides direction whilst allowing people the latitude to find their own creative ways of achieving the overall goal, giving the change process added momentum. Branding also makes it easier to use classic sales and marketing techniques to heighten awareness of change through things like posters and internal newsletters. Any brand requires investment of resources to get it off the ground and it can be undermined by negative experiences and bad publicity. However, through extensive marketing a brand starts to become familiar and accepted, eventually entering the language and going mainstream.

7.6   The influence of leaders

How do you lead a swarm of bees? The answer is simple, just find the queen bee and the rest will follow. If only change at work was that simple! Just find the equivalent of a queen bee, persuade her to change and everyone else will follow. It is tempting with organisations to think that if the CEO is on board then the whole organisation will follow. If this were the case then change would be a good deal easier to manage (and this book would be redundant).

However, a trusted Chief Executive or other senior executive who is genuinely passionate about a change will certainly be able to create momentum of her own. She will be able to ensure that resources are deployed in support of the change and can use internal and external communication channels to promote her vision. But she also needs the active support of other directors with authority over the areas that will be most affected by the change. They in turn need to gain the support of their direct reports, and so on all the way down to team leaders.

As we have seen in every chapter of this book, leaders at all levels have a pivotal role to play in every aspect of successful change. Through the loyalty and trust of subordinates or through dint of positional power they can sway the opinions of large groups of people. Their enthusiastic backing will be vital in galvanising support for change.

Leaders at every level in an organisation have a good deal of influence over their teams, so positive leadership is required from all leaders for a smooth change to come about. It is unquestionably true that where leaders of any operating unit, department or team oppose a change then their team will almost inevitably oppose it also. If leaders are displaying dysfunctional behaviour, you can bet that their team will behave likewise.

Where departmental leaders are Late Adopters or Laggards it is as well, where possible, to leave off changing their department until after others have been converted. This enables them to be swayed by the successes achieved elsewhere in the organisation and to feel the peer pressure of feeling left out.

For organisational change to take root, leaders must be passionate champions of change. They need to understand how to distinguish between Early Adopters and Laggards amongst the leaders that report to them so that they can convert a critical mass of them to the cause and tip the balance in favour of change.

Summary

Change is scary and exciting at the same time. By working with different people according to their enthusiasm and acceptance of change, it is possible to build initial momentum for change and then to use peer pressure (as well as the 5 Forces of Change) to build critical mass and tip the balance of opinion in favour of change.

Leaders should:

1. Ensure that the Chief Executive and/or other senior executives (with authority over the people most affected by the change) provides passionate advocacy for the change.

2. Create consensus amongst the senior leadership team for change.

3. Task senior leaders with winning over leaders within their own teams.

4. Recruit Innovators and Early Adopters onto the change team to provide some initial energy and impetus to the change. Look for people who are widely respected and are natural networkers to spread the messages about change.

5. Convert some members of the Early Majority or Late Majority to credible ambassadors for change.

6. Where possible leave the Late Majority and Laggards out of the first phase of change.

7. Publicise early successes following the change.

8. Brand your change and use sales and marketing techniques to create awareness and acceptance of the change further fuelling peer pressure.

Chapter 8

Preparing for Change

8.1 Assessing your change

Before embarking on a major change, it is wise to gauge how prepared your organisation is for the change and to plan accordingly. You should also pinpoint the main obstacles and pinch points associated with the change, allowing you to focus your attention and resources where they are most needed. This also enables you to make decisions about how you design and implement the change to increase your level of success.

How difficult it will be to implement a change successfully depends on two main factors; firstly, the **Degree of Difficultly** of the change itself (i.e. how much it is likely to trigger negative reactions from the people it affects) and, secondly, the **Adaptability to Change** of your organisation and its people (i.e. how well set up your organisation is to manage change and to accept change from a cultural perspective). Is the change, for instance, similar to something you've done successfully in the past and easy to implement using your existing robust approach to delivering change? On the other hand, is it a countercultural change in an organisation that views all change with suspicion? Whatever the case, you should be wary of any change that is labelled 'simple' until you have assessed it properly.

This chapter provides some practical tools for assessing the difficulty of a change and the readiness of your organisation to absorb it. It also highlights what you can do to permanently increase your organisation's ability to deal effectively with change.

8.2 Degree of difficulty of the change

So what are the characteristics of a change that make it harder or easier to achieve? Answering this question is a relatively straightforward task once you have an appreciation of the 5 Forces of Change. Simply put, if the change causes no uncertainty, is entirely within people's own control, breaks no connections, is fully aligned with the organisations purpose and values, and will not undermine people's ability to succeed, then the Degree of Difficulty of the change will be zero and it should go through without a hitch. To make a complete assessment of the ease with which a change can be implemented, the Degree of Difficulty of the change has to be combined with an understanding of the Adaptability to Change of the organisation in question (see section 8.3).

Taking each of the 5 Forces of Change in turn, you can evaluate the Degree of Difficulty of a change by conducting an analysis of the change using the survey below. In the very early stage of a change it may be difficult to answer some of these questions accurately, but they will still highlight areas of concern and prompt you to take the appropriate action.

This survey can be completed by people across the organisation to give you an understanding of how the change is perceived by others and to highlight issues that will need to be addressed. It may also be possible to use the feedback to redesign the change to reduce the Degree of Difficulty and make it more user-friendly.

Please feel free to use this and other surveys in this book within your own organisation.

Degree of Difficulty Survey

Strongly Disagree — 0 1 2 3 4 5 — Strongly Agree

Score the following statements from 0 – 5, where 0 means you "strongly disagree" and 5 means you "strongly agree".

As there are 20 questions, the maximum score for a change is 100 (supremely difficult) and the minimum score is zero (supremely easy).

Certainty

1. This is a large-scale change which will have a big effect on people.
2. There will be a long period of transition while the change is implemented.
3. The way the change will take place is unclear.
4. There is no clear and confident leadership of the change.

Purpose

5. The change goes against the current culture (i.e. it conflicts with the current purpose and values* of the organisation).
6. The change goes against the values of people within the organisation.
7. The purpose for the change is unclear.
8. Keeping things as they are would be an easy, painless option.

*a common set of beliefs about how we should do things and how we should work with each other and with our customers, suppliers and the wider community

Control

9. Decisions about the nature of the change are outside the hands of those affected (e.g. it is imposed from above or from a distance).
10. People affected by change have not been involved in or consulted about what the change will be or how it will happen.

11. There has been little two-way communication about the change.
12. There is little flexibility for team and people to decide how to implement the change in their own areas.

Connection

13. People feel overall that they will lose out due to the change.
14. The way people work has remained unchanged for a long time.
15. The way people carry out their work will change significantly.
16. The way people work with other people will change significantly.

Success

17. People will need to master a lot of new skills to be successful after the change.
18. People will need to make a big shift in their attitudes and behaviours to be successful after the change.
19. People's goals and targets will need to change significantly following the change.
20. It is unclear what people need to do to be considered successful after the change.

The higher the score on this survey, the greater the degree of difficulty associated with that force. This is best illustrated by the following example.

Imagine the following scenario. An organisation is going through a major restructure to organise itself according to the customers it serves rather than structuring itself according to internal functions. Instead of having a series of operational departments plus marketing, finance, HR etc. it will be divided up into business units dedicated to different types of customer. Each business unit will carry out its own operations, marketing, HR etc. There will be a loose connection between business units. There will be a very lean corporate unit to coordinate the activities of the business units which will be largely autonomous. Previously, the organisation had been very hierarchical and only sales and marketing dealt with customers. Now, heads of each business unit will be expected to run these business units as if they were separate businesses and everyone will be encouraged to think about their work from the customer's perspective rather than a functional perspective. People's daily tasks will remain very much the same though teams will be split up amongst the business units.

The change has been announced by the new CEO (who joined the company 6 months ago) as the new 'Customer First' initiative whereby the company will reverse declining sales through industry-leading customer service. He has also set out a clear vision for regaining the companies pre-eminence in the industry over the next three years.

There has been a lot of rumour about change, but the announcement surprised many people, even those in senior positions. A dedicated project team, made up of highly capable and respected individuals, is in place led by the operations director who has enthusiastically endorsed the change and set out a clear timetable for the transition to take place within four months. He has also embarked on a series of breakfast meetings across the company to explain how the company's long history of dedication to quality needs to be augmented with a greater focus on customers who have been let down in the past and who are taking their business to the competition. He also wants to forge stronger links with suppliers in the race to be the most flexible and efficient company in the industry. He has been very open about the difficulties of change and welcomed feedback from the people at all levels.

There is some excitement in the company about getting clear direction after the organisation has drifted for a number of years. There is some concern about the extent of the change and what it means for people, though there have been reassurances about no job losses. There is some scepticism about certain business unit managers being able to lead the new business units effectively as if they were standalone businesses.

Figure 8.1 illustrates the score you might expect from the Degree of Difficulty Survey for such a change. Each of the 5 Forces of Change can be scored up to a maximum of 20 (adding together the scores for the 4 relevant questions) where 20 indicates a very high degree of difficulty associated with that force.

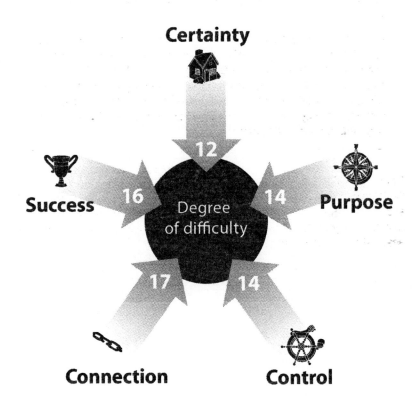

*Figure 8.1   Example of Force Field Analysis of the Degree of
Difficulty of a change*

Certainty

This is an ambitious and far-reaching change. However, the vision and plan set out by leadership team is clear and backed up by the visible enthusiasm of the operations director, and so Certainty scores 12.

Purpose

The purpose of the change has been set out clearly and linked to the company's purpose, but there is a new emphasis on the customer as well as quality, which represents an important change, so Purpose scores 14.

Control

The change has been thought up by the new CEO and some of the leadership team and dictated from on high. However, the Operations Director has been doing a good job of communicating the change openly and taking people's views on board, so Control scores 14 out of 20.

Connection

Whilst people's jobs will remain largely intact, teams will be broken up across the organisation and people are being asked to work differently with customers and suppliers, so Connection scores 17.

Success

Most people will experience little change to their daily routine but there is a new attitude required to serve customers better. Many senior managers will need to make a major change to the way they work as they get to grips with running autonomous businesses, so Success scores 16.

Overall, the change scores 73 out of 100, making it a difficult change. All 5 Forces of Change will need to be addressed but Connection and Success will need the greatest attention.

8.3 Organisational adaptability to change

The second factor that will help you determine your approach to a given change is the **Adaptability to Change** of your organisation and its people, i.e. the ability of the organisation and its people to absorb change quickly and effectively. The 5 Forces of Change can once again be used to work out where you stand. The series of questions listed below will help you to assess the extent to which your organisation's structures, processes, culture, etc., facilitate or impede change. They will also help you identify areas of concern and to plan how best to work within current constraints. The higher the overall score, the higher the Adaptability to Change of the organisation and its people and the greater the likelihood of successful change.

Organisation Adaptability to Change Survey

Strongly Disagree

Strongly Agree

0   1   2   3   4   5

Score the following statements from 0 - 5, where 0 means you "strongly disagree" and 5 means you "strongly agree".

As there are 20 questions, the maximum score for an organisation is 100 (supremely adaptable to change) and the minimum score is zero (supremely inflexible to change).

Certainty

1. Leaders and managers have a good understanding of how to make change work in practice and lead by example.
2. Resources and processes are in place to manage projects / change effectively.
3. There is open and effective communication up, down and across the organisation.
4. The organisation and its people are happy to take risks.

Purpose

5. There is a strong sense of purpose in the organisation.
6. There are strong shared values in the organisation (i.e. there is a common set of beliefs about how we should do things and how we should work together and with or customers and suppliers and the wider community).
7. Progress against company strategy is regularly communicated.
8. Shared values are regularly reinforced by managers and executives.

Control

9. People are allowed to make decisions for themselves and take action in their part of the organisation.
10. There is little or no hierarchy in the organisation.

11. There is a history of consulting widely with people before major decisions are taken.
12. There is a history of explaining to people why major decisions have been made.

Connection

13. Working practices change regularly (i.e. they have not been ingrained over many years).
14. Internal relationships (the way we work together) and external relationships (the way we work with customers and/or suppliers) change regularly.
15. The organisation has a good track record of successful change in the past.
16. People are happy to change the way they do things.

Success

17. There is a strong tradition of learning new skills and ways of working in the organisation.
18. There is a strong tradition of learning lessons from the past and improving performance within the organisation.
19. People are recognised and rewarded for their contribution to the organisation.
20. People are given regular feedback on their performance.

Continuing with our example of an organisation going through a restructure, it is helpful to consider how the company might score on Adaptability to Change. To do this, it helps to know a bit more about the organisation.

The company has been in business for fifty years and has been through a number of ups and downs. Throughout its history it has had a strong brand and been regarded as 'the one to beat' in the industry. It is also the training ground for many people in the industry given its consistent investment in developing its people. In general, managers are adept at coaching their teams and recognising them for good performance. People who work for the company are loyal and proud of its dedication to quality and strong reputation for looking after its people. Some see it as overly paternalistic and hierarchical. Communication up and down the organisation has been limited historically, though the new leadership team has taken steps to turn this situation around. In past years, it has been slow to change, but has recently been through a major IT systems overhaul which has been very successful. The overhaul made a significant difference to the way people work.

Figure 8.2 illustrates the score that you might expect this organisation to achieve for Adaptability to Change.

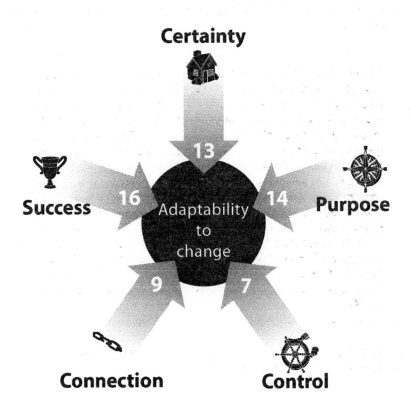

Figure 8.2   Example of Force Field Analysis of the Adaptability to Change of an organisation

Certainty

The organisation is quite slow to change but has got an infrastructure in place to manage change. Leaders are willing to set direction and lead by example, so Certainty scores 13 out of 20 (where a score of 20 would mean that it handles uncertainty extremely well).

Purpose

The company has a clear purpose and strong shared values, so the score for Purpose is 14.

Control

The organisation is quite hierarchical and historically has not consulted with its people about change, so for Control it scores 7 out of 20.

Connection

Internal and external relationships have remained unchanged for many years though work practices have recently changed significantly due to the introduction of new technology (which also set a precedent for successful organisational change) so Connection scores 9.

Success

There is a strong ethos of personal development including coaching by managers, so for Success the score is 16.

The overall Adaptability to Change of the organisation is 59, which means that whilst it is not highly adaptable it does have a degree of flexibility. All 5 Forces of Change will need to be addressed, but Control and Connection are the weakest areas and so will need the greatest attention.

8.4   Readiness for change

Readiness for Change is the measure of a given organisation's ability to deliver a specific change successfully. It combines the Degree of Difficulty of the change with the Adaptability to Change of the organisation in question.

If you are embarking on a change with a low Degree of Difficulty in an organisation with a high Adaptability to Change you are most likely to get a successful outcome. On the other hand, a change with a high Degree of Difficulty in an organisation with a low Adaptability to Change is going to require a lot of drive and ingenuity, and perhaps a good deal of time, to succeed. In such a case, you may decide that the change should not be attempted in its current form or left until such time as the organisation is in a better position to take it on board.

One Process Improvement Team I worked with, which was responsible for manufacturing efficiency improvement at a global food manufacturer, always assessed the change readiness of its factories before initiating a project. It would not attempt an efficiency improvement project if the factory (and in particular its leadership team) was not ready to improve.

Figure 8.3 illustrates how considering the Degree of Difficulty of a change alongside an organisation's Adaptability to Change is important in understanding how you might approach a given change or a portfolio of changes. At one extreme, a change with a low Degree of Difficulty in a highly adaptable organisation can be thought of as straightforward and should go through with little fuss. At the other extreme, some major changes in highly inflexible organisations should only be undertaken if there really is very little choice but to change. In such cases, the best approach is to 'loosen up' the organisation before embarking on change as described in Section 8.4. Highly adaptable organisations can afford to take on changes with a very high Degree of Difficulty, provided that the benefits are high and resources are available to make it happen (i.e. there are not too many ambitious changes going on at the same time). Finally, where the Degree of Difficulty is low but the organisation has a low Adaptability to Change, it is necessary to focus your resources on overcoming organisational weaknesses such as instigating a comprehensive campaign of communication where, historically, information flow has been poor.

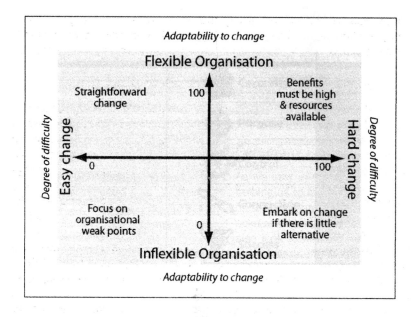

Figure 8.3   Illustration of Change Readiness

8.5   Increasing the adaptability of your organisation

Any organisation that can change frequently and effortlessly is well set up for success in the 21st Century. In an ever-changing environment, it is the organisations that can innovate and change faster than the rest that will survive and prosper in the long run.

Can a large, inflexible organisation make itself more change-friendly? Can it learn to flex and bend or even transform itself as it needs to? The answer to these questions is 'yes', though it may require a fundamental shift in culture and take some time to achieve. Certainly, those organisations that train their people, especially their leaders, in the principles of effective change management will eliminate many of the difficulties associated with major change.

Listed below are some actions that organisations can take to increase their Adaptability to Change. Some can be carried out quite quickly whilst others, requiring more fundamental change, will take a good deal longer.

How you go about increasing the Adaptability to Change of your organisation depends on your starting point. If your organisation is already well set up for change, some of the actions listed here may be redundant.

1. Educate leaders in the art of leading change

Educating executives and managers in how to lead change (by harnessing the 5 Forces of Change) is perhaps the single most efficient and effective way of boosting an organisation's adaptability. If leaders can be motivated and equipped to lead change from the front, to engage in open communication, to empower their people and to support and encourage them through the ups and downs of organisational change, there is every chance that the change will succeed. Leaders who appreciate the consequences of change also tend to design and implement change in a more user-friendly manner.

Leaders are, of course, only human. They are prone to the same forces that hold people back from embracing major change, so converting them to the cause of a given change is just as important as developing their skills in leading change. By educating leaders about change you can, in fact, achieve the twin goals of increasing their personal tolerance for change (through their deeper appreciation of the change process) whilst enhancing their ability to lead others through change.

2. Develop an understanding of change throughout the organisation

The first step in helping people deal with change is to help them appreciate why change can be difficult for them. If they understand the 5 Forces of Change they will not be surprised when they feel anxious or frustrated and will realise that it is just part and parcel of the change process and that it is ok, for instance, to struggle with letting go of the old ways of doing things. They will also have a common language with which to express their frustrations or deal with issues. For example, they can ask their leaders questions about what constitutes success after the change or request a degree of autonomy in implementing the change in their own way. You will find that once this understanding of change exists across your organisation, people will feel far more in control of the situation and more relaxed about the transition process. In short, you can find yourself pushing at an open door rather than battering on a locked one.

3. Establish open communication

Open communication is critical to helping people feel involved in change (rather than victims of change). It helps people understand the purpose of change as well as its benefits and shortcomings. Regular, open and honest communication breeds trust, increases certainty and so reduces anxiety.

Instituting a range of communication mechanisms into the daily life of your organisation and building a culture of open two-way communication is one of the most important factors in developing Adaptability to Change. Poor communication means people come to rely on rumour and assume that the leadership team is actively hiding things from them; a recipe for mistrust, especially during times of change.

4. Establish project discipline

Any major change requires effective project management if it is to be delivered with a minimum number of glitches. Good project management ensures that the efforts of different people are coordinated efficiently, that issues and risks are identified and dealt with appropriately and that the whole effort is overseen and steered by the right group of senior leaders. Good project managers will build elements of change management into their plans, such as ongoing communication with stakeholders and post-implementation support. Having strong project discipline enables you to build up a track record of successful change, increasing levels of trust amongst those affected and reducing levels of uncertainty and anxiety.

5. Establish a culture of learning and development

For some people the very idea of learning something new, especially in a formal environment such as a training room, makes them feel they are being sent back to school or implies to them that they are somehow not good enough at their job. Others view it as 'a day off work'. Organisations that habitually develop their people can overcome these prejudices and establish a culture where people expect to learn and to improve their performance. So when a change comes along, the process of learning new skills and behaviours will be a straightforward and familiar one.

At an organisational level, a culture of learning means that organisations are willing and able to reflect on past failures and successes and systematically improve performance based on the lessons they have learnt. Very often, failures are either brushed aside as unfortunate incidents that are best forgotten or they become the focus for blame. Whereas organisations that recognise failures as important opportunities to learn and improve reduce their odds of making mistakes in the future. It is more surprising, perhaps, that successes are also prone to be forgotten in the rush to the next challenge. People and organisations that learn systematically from their successes and failures will learn something new from every change they encounter (through a process of group post-implementation review) and increase their collective skill at bringing about change.

6. Establish performance management

As we have seen, even after a change has been launched people may still choose not change. They may not adopt new customer service principles or follow new, more efficient, working practices. They may not use the new computer system to its full potential or accept their role in the new organisation structure. So if you want to realise the benefits of change you need to spend time after it been launched embedding it into the organisation. Perhaps the most important tool at your disposal for doing this is performance management.

If people are aware of the targets they have to achieve and the behaviours they need to demonstrate to achieve them, and managers hold people to account and coach them to improve, then you have an effective performance management system in place. When change comes about, it is then a relatively straightforward matter to educate people about changed behaviours and new targets, and for managers to support them in adopting these new behaviours to achieve the new targets.

7. Establish purpose and values

As we saw in Chapter 6, a strong sense of purpose and a well established set of values give people a sense of certainty (even control) during times of great change. Where these are lacking, it requires a strong determination at the most senior level, not to mention a large amount of time and effort, to establish them. However, organisations that do establish a strong sense of identity and robust culture have been shown to be far more successful in the long run than organisations that do not (see *Built to Last* by James Collins and Jerry Porras). This is not surprising as these organisations have what it takes to weather the storms that beset any organisation that lasts any substantial length of time.

8. Empowerment

People at the top of a hierarchical organisation are often comfortable with the idea of major change. After all, they have been party to the discussions leading up to the change and have made the decision to go ahead with it. They tend to worry more about whether their managers and staff will implement their decision and are sometimes baffled when their enthusiasm for a particular initiative is not reflected by others lower down the organisation.

In empowering organisations, people are trusted and expected to make decisions for themselves and take action accordingly. They are given ownership of change and so there is less tendency for people to feel like victims of it. In these empowered organisations people cannot rely on their boss to tell them exactly what to so they are used to using their initiative to tackle novel situations. Thus, breaking down organisational hierarchy and increasing empowerment makes people and organisations more adaptable to change.

9. Establishing change as the corm

Small entrepreneurial organisations with a clear sense of purpose, where everything is new and everyone mucks in together can often outmanoeuvre their slower more ponderous and risk-averse competitors. In these organisations, change is accepted as a necessary part of growth. Successful changes are celebrated and failures are used as an opportunity to learn how to succeed next time. Risk is not used as an automatic excuse to do nothing, nor is it ignored. Rather, it is managed as best as possible.

This is not a picture that people in larger, more mature organisations are likely to recognise. They find that their organisation is not in the habit of changing, and they have to kick and scream to get new ideas introduced. There is fear of risk, leading to slow decision-making and the avoidance of any sort of danger. Rather than responding nimbly to changes in the environment, their organisation has become arthritic and as a consequence finds itself failing to keep up with the times.

Like humans, organisations need regular exercise to remain fit and nimble. Rather than doing stretching exercises and going for regular workouts at the gym, organisations need regular change to build up their flexibility and endurance. It is only by practicing change that people and organisations can become accustomed to it. Eventually, change becomes the accepted norm and people take it in their stride.

Summary

The 5 Forces of Change provide a simple framework for assessing the Degree of Difficulty of a change and for assessing an organisation's Adaptability to Change. These assessments will tell you where to focus your efforts in leading change.

Combining the Degree of Difficulty with Adaptability to Change indicates an organisation's Readiness for Change for a given initiative and helps to gauge the overall effort required to deliver a change successfully.

Organisations can take action to improve their adaptability to change. The easiest and most productive place to start is to educate leaders in how to lead change. Other strategies, such as increasing levels of empowerment in the organisation, may take a lot more time and effort to implement.

Chapter 9

Implementing Change

9.1 Introduction

This chapter brings together the ideas covered in previous chapters and translates them into practical guidance on the best way to implement your change initiative. It examines how people's responses to change shift over the lifecycle of a change and introduces a collection of tools and techniques that will assist you in harnessing the 5 Forces of Change.

9.2 Three phases of change

It helps to think about change in three broad phases.

Phase 1, the *Pre-Change Phase*, involves the build up to change when it is planned and designed, and people first learn about what is going to happen. The role of a leader in this phase is to increase people's sense of certainty and control by, for instance, setting out a clear purpose and plan for change linked to the organisation's purpose, strategy and values.

Phase 2, the *Transition Phase*, is the period during which people learn what they need to do and start adapting to the new world before it becomes reality. This is a time when people need detailed information about what is expected of them and when training plays a key role in developing the skills and behaviours required for people to be successful. It is also a time to let go of old connections and develop new ones.

Phase 3, the *Post-Change Phase*, is when the change is implemented and needs to be embedded into the organisation. This is when coaching and performance management play a crucial role in locking in change and preventing people from backsliding into old habits. It is also the point at which to review what has happened and to learn from successes and failures. This phase is often overlooked by people who believe (incorrectly) that the change process ends with transition or when people's attention switches to the next big change initiative.

There is an emotional roller-coaster ride that takes people successfully or otherwise from Phase 1 to Phase 3. The ride is different for different people and different parts of the organisation according to how they are affected and their attitude to change. It is likely that some people, especially those involved closely with defining and organising the change, may well have finished the ride ahead of the majority of the population, whereas others may only come on board long after the change appears to be over and done with. The task is to get everyone (or as many people as possible) to come out at the other end ready to move on.

9.3   Responding positively or negatively to change

The emotions that people feel as they progress through change have been the subject of this book so far. The 5 Forces of Change affect people differently during each of the three phases of the change journey.

People's response to the 5 Forces of Change depends on who they are, how the change is managed and the stage of the change in which they find themselves. Where people are not well disposed to change or where change is poorly managed, typical responses include fright (anxiety about change), flight (avoiding the change), and fight (opposing the change). People can and do opt out even when they appear to have made it through to Phase 3. At the opposite end of the spectrum, where people understand change and feel engaged in it, there is eager anticipation of change, a desire to get involved and enthusiastic support for its success.

Where people perceive that they will largely lose out due to a change, it is not automatically the case that they will respond negatively. Where they feel truly engaged in the change they can come to understand that the change is necessary to the organisation's long term success and to accept that they need to make some sacrifice. Equally, people may react badly to a change even though an objective assessment would indicate that it will be beneficial to them. It may be that they feel no ownership of the change or they are so reluctant to let go of the past that the benefits of change are not enough to persuade people to get on board.

Some examples of how people can and do respond negatively and positively to each of the 5 Forces of Change in each of the three phases of a change are set out in Figure 9.1 below. This table illustrates the huge gulf between a poorly managed change in an inflexible organisation which elicits negative responses to change and well managed change in a highly adaptable organisation which elicits positive responses. The one feels like an uphill battle, the other like sailing with the wind at your back. It is the difference between meeting the 5 Forces of Change head on and harnessing them to drive change forward.

Figure 9.1 illustrates that people's questions and concerns evolve over the lifetime of a change and so the focus of your effort in leading change needs to evolve as well. In the case of Success, for instance, prior to the change it may be all about building confidence in greater success in the future; during transition it may be about ensuring the best possible training; and post-implementation it may be about coaching people and recognising success.

This shift of emphasis through the lifecycle of a change is illustrated in the table below. It shows, for instance, that conveying a strong sense of purpose and giving people control is essential in the early stages of a change, whilst creating new connections and reinforcing success is more important in the middle to latter stages. The tools and techniques you apply will likewise change at different points in the lifecycle.

5 Forces	Phase 1 Pre-Change	Phase 2 Transition	Phase 3 Post-Change
Certainty			
Negative response	Anxiety about an uncertain future and potential loss	Anxiety due to a time of flux and insecurity about being able to meet new expectations	Anxiety caused by difficulties in adjusting to new circumstance
Positive response	Excitement and hope about the prospects of a better future	Excitement at trying out something new	Confidence from a clear view of new expectations and being equipped to succeed
Purpose			
Negative response	Confusion about direction and purpose	Loss of direction as things begin to change	Diminished sense of purpose
Positive response	Understanding of the change in the context of the organisations purpose and values	Sense of overall direction despite things beginning to change	A renewed sense of purpose
Control			
Negative response	Frustration at the lack of consultation and the prospect of adapting to something outside of your control	Reluctance to learn new skills and behaviours imposed from outside	Reluctance to stick to new 'foreign' practices

Positive response	A feeling of engagement in bringing about change	A desire to get involved and make the change a success	A feeling of ownership for any successes and a desire to correct any shortcomings

Connection

Negative response	Distress at anticipated loss of old ways and old relationships	Difficulty with or inability to let go of the old in favour of the new	Nostalgia for or reversion to the old ways
Positive response	Belief that loss is a price worth paying	Welcoming the new and letting go of the past (without denigrating it)	Rapid connection to new ways and new relationships

Success

Negative response	Fear of potential failure	Confusion about what will constitute success and a reluctance to learn new practices	Loss of confidence due to early failures
Positive response	Anticipation of greater success in the future	Satisfaction of mastering new techniques and new skills	Increased self-esteem from initial successes and recognition by others

Figure 9.1   Positive and Negative Responses to Change

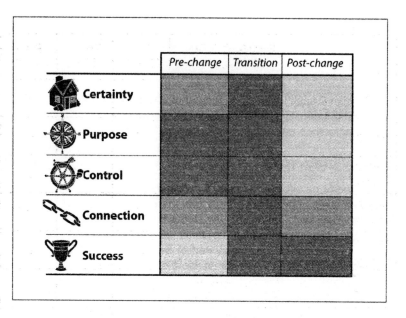

	Pre-change	Transition	Post-change
Certainty			
Purpose			
Control			
Connection			
Success			

Figure 9.2 Emphasis of change leadership effort over time (the darker the shading, the greater the focus of leadership effort)

9.4 Tools and techniques for implementing change

Throughout this book, we have seen how various tools and techniques can be used to harness the forces of change or to counteract their negative effects. This section gathers together a number of these tools and techniques and shows how they can be applied over the lifetime of a change and how many of them address more than one of the 5 Forces of Change. Once the Degree of Difficulty of the change and the Adaptability to Change of your organisation are known (see Chapter 8), you can select the tools and techniques that will be most effective in dealing with likely problem areas and shortcomings.

The table in Figure 9.3 lists a number of tools and techniques that support the successful implementation of change indicating which of the 5 Forces of Change each one addresses and in which phase of the change it should generally be applied. A description of how to apply each tool or technique then follows.

	Force(s) Chiefly Addressed	Pre-Change	Trans-ition	Post-Change
Communication	Primary: Certainty Secondary: All others	✓	✓	✓
Branding	Primary: Purpose Secondary: Connection	✓	✓	✓
Project Management	Primary: Certainty Secondary: Control	✓	✓	✓
Stakeholder Management	Primary: Control Secondary: Certainty	✓	✓	✓
Change Champions	Primary: Certainty Secondary: Connection	✓	✓	✓
Piloting	Primary: Certainty Secondary: Control	✓		
Consultation	Primary: Control Secondary: Certainty	✓	✓	
Engagement Events	Primary: Control Secondary: Connection	✓	✓	
Timeline	Primary: Connection Secondary: Purpose	✓	✓	
Ceremony	Primary: Connection Secondary: Certainty		✓	
Celebrating Success	Primary: Success Secondary: Certainty		✓	✓
Training & Development	Primary: Success Secondary: Control		✓	✓
Performance Management	Primary: Success Secondary: Purpose		✓	✓
Lessons Learned Review	Primary: All Secondary: N/A			✓

Figure 9.3 Tools and techniques for leading change during different stages of the change lifecycle

Communication

An effective campaign of communication is crucial to aspects of a successful change. It helps build certainty and enhances people's sense of control (through knowledge and dialogue). It is vital in building a sense of purpose for the change, publicising success and building connection to new practices and new teams. See Section 2.6 for more detail on communication.

Branding

When you are embarking on an important change that requires people to think in new ways, branding the initiative can help in a variety of ways.

Manufacturers and retailers are keenly aware of how people connect with brands, creating loyalty to the products they sell. So it is that people connect with a change initiative if it is well marketed. As we saw in Chapter 6, Marks and Spencer have branded their ambitious plans to be carbon neutral by 2012 as Plan A. This has helped them to infiltrate the initiative into every aspect of the organisation and outward to their suppliers, their customers and the general public creating brand awareness and brand loyalty.

Branding helps simplify communication of the purpose change. For instance, a drive to reduce manufacturing errors which is branded as 'Squeaky Clean' allows people to communicate simply that their objective is to get their production line squeaky clean or that they have a number of squeaky clean projects on the go. Squeaky clean notices can be posted up with advice on improving quality. It can even encourage people to take the initiative and to set up their own squeaky clean sessions to brainstorm new ideas for improving quality. After a while it enters into the language and becomes the norm. People are set squeaky clean targets, receive squeaky clean awards and even talk to their suppliers and customers about it.

Project management

Project management is essential to the effective delivery of change. Without project management the change will not be delivered effectively. Good project management discipline is also an important factor in keeping people motivated through change. People gain great confidence and certainty from clear project plans (see Chapter 2) and a professionally organised project team. During the transition period it is particularly important that people experience a well executed plan. A great plan well executed will also minimise the 'teething problems' that typically follow change, increasing levels success and boosting the adoption of new practices. Good project management is also about supporting people in carrying out new practices beyond the transition period, helping to ensure that change is embedded in the organisation.

Where projects can go wrong is in assuming that management of change is just another set of tasks to be completed on the project plan. Whilst it is important to plan activities such as communication and stakeholder management, change should not be viewed as simply a sub-component of a project. Otherwise, it can be seen as strictly the preserve of those responsible for carrying out 'change management' tasks and can easily be cut back on should resources become tight.

A better way of looking at it is that the role of project managers is to help organisations bring about change. This shifts people's perspective from completing project tasks and meeting project deadlines to the delivering significant change, involving new attitudes and behaviours as well as new processes, systems, structures and roles.

Stakeholder management

Stakeholder management is about ensuring that everyone affected by change is given as much control over the change as is practically possible, as was described in Sections 3.6 and 3.7, this includes everything from giving people the chance to voice their concerns to involving them in designing and implementing change.

Change champions

As we saw in Chapter 7, some people will be natural enthusiasts for any given change. If these people are tasked with galvanising support across the business they can help create a groundswell of positive opinion that eventually tips the balance in favour of change. Whilst these champions of change may already be early adopters their enthusiasm and active participation in change can persuade other less enthusiastic colleagues to come on board.

Piloting

Piloting a change by testing it out in one small part of the organisation before rolling out elsewhere is a common approach to reducing the risks associated with change. It affords an opportunity to learn through trial and error and iron out any problems. We saw in Chapter 4, for instance, how

Jamie Oliver worked initially with one school to learn the ins and outs of improving school meals before taking on the schools across an entire region of the country. The downside of piloting a change is that it can encourage lengthy trials slowing the change process down and prolonging the period of uncertainty within the organisation. However, it is very useful in providing evidence that the change can work in practice, giving people greater confidence in the process. Also, people who have been through the change become highly credible spokespeople who can advise others about the best way to implement the change and to allay their fears about the future.

Consultation

Consultation involves talking to stakeholders about your plans for change and gathering their opinions on the way the change should be structured and/or implemented. If this seems blindingly obvious then it's because, in fact, it is. However, people give a range of reasons for avoiding it. These include "There isn't enough time", "People may suggest things we don't want to do" and "If they find out what we plan to do they will become distracted or unhappy". All of these excuses are used time and again to ensure that consultation does not take place, with the result that people are kept in the dark and excluded from the process. As a consequence, uncertainty increases and people's sense of control diminishes, endangering the change. We saw in Chapter 3 what happened when parents were not consulted about the change to school lunches – they passed burgers and chips through the school railings undermining the whole initiative.

Consultation does not have to be arduous. You can, for instance, consult representative groups of people through a series of structured workshops rather than conferring with every single person. Whilst it does take some time and effort to consult people properly, it is nowhere near as onerous as having to unravel the consequences of plotting change in isolation. People will point out all sorts of things you had not thought of and give you a sense of how easily accepted the change will be.

If a decision has been made to go ahead with a change come what may, do not consult with people falsely on whether or not the change should go ahead but simply on how best to make it happen. Honesty is the key to success. Set out the situation clearly and gather opinions appropriately.

If there is a concern that a change is going to make people nervous or unhappy, there is all the more reason to consult with them early and often. Better to engage people in an adult manner rather than keeping them in the dark and risking major upset when the change is suddenly and unexpectedly revealed.

Consultation is of greatest use in Phase 1, Pre-Change, but can be continued into Phase 2 when you can consult with people on how best to implement a given change.

Engagement events

Engagement events are mass interactive communication events (known by some as Town Hall Meetings). Their aim is not just to tell people about change but to engage them more deeply in the whys and wherefores of change. Typically, they involve a series of experiences that deal with different aspects of change. These meetings are usually set out like exhibition halls with a series of stands manned by different people (preferably senior stakeholders). People move from stand to stand in small groups and at each one the "exhibitors" lead them through an activity, such as a discussion on how their roles will change or an exercise in working out how the change will help them meet changing customer needs. There may also be opportunities to contribute to how the change is implemented. One helpful technique is to present the history and circumstances surrounding the decision to embark on change and allow people to work through the same decision-making process for themselves. This is far more powerful in helping people understand and internalise the change than merely explaining it to them.

People invariably leave such events feeling far more certain of the future and whilst they may not feel they can greatly influence the change, they do have a greater sense of control over it by having had the opportunity to fully digest it. Town Hall Meetings can be used in Phase 1 and Phase 2 to engage people in the build up to implementing the change and to gather feedback from people as to how best to implement it.

Timeline technique

A powerful technique that can be employed in a range of circumstances, such as in consultation workshops or in a Town Hall Meeting, is the timeline process described in detail in Chapter 4. It involves plotting key events in the organisation's history leading up to change and into the future when the change has already taken place. It allows people to gain a new perspective on change by looking at it in the context of other changes that have happened in the past. It allows issues in the past, present and future to be brought to the surface and to be dealt with explicitly as objective problems rather than rumbling around in the background causing discontent. Seen in context, the current change becomes less frightening and people become less worried once they have had a chance to voice their concerns. It helps them to begin the process of breaking their connection with past practices and past loyalties and to start building connections to the ways of the future. The timeline technique is ideally used in Phase 1, but it can be used in Phase 2 right up to the point where people are being trained in new skills and behaviours (though it is preferable to tackle people's concerns far earlier than this).

Ceremony

As we saw in Chapter 4, ceremony plays an important part in our lives, helping us to mark important events and to ease the process of letting go of the past and embracing the future. Like wakes, ceremonies at work acknowledge loss, celebrate past triumphs and lay the past to rest. They also look forward to new opportunities and to new triumphs. They are a powerful route to breaking old connections and initiating new ones.

This point is illustrated well by the example of two high schools that were in the process of merging. Students from each high school collected together objects that represented their school (school ties, school magazines, prayer books etc.) and sealed them in two time capsules. These time capsules were then bricked into the walls of a new library being built for the new merged school and left for generations to come.

Celebrate success

Celebrating early wins following a change is important in helping to build up positive PR for the change and to encourage late adopters of change to get on board (see Chapter 6). Having senior leaders publicly recognise individuals and teams for adopting the change is one important way of doing this. Creating new stories about what it takes to be successful is a powerful way of shifting an organisation's culture.

Another simple technique is to set a series of highly visible short-term, medium-term and long-term targets so that incremental success can be publicly celebrated, boosting morale on a regular basis and maintaining the change's momentum.

Training and development

Developing new skills and behaviours is vital to the success of any change. But developing people takes time and often entails taking them away from their daily duties for days on end. All too often, it is seen as a necessary evil to be carried out with a minimum of disruption to operations.

However, high quality training and development boosts people's confidence and ability to succeed following the change, increasing their degree of certainty and sense of control over their work. It provides opportunities to bring new teams together to develop new connections. It also represents a golden opportunity to win over people's hearts and minds by engaging them in a vision of a brighter future.

There is an optimal time for developing people, and that is just ahead of the moment when they need the new skills and behaviours to succeed. Nothing focuses the mind better than the thought that what you are about to learn needs to be applied in work the next day or the next week. Train people too soon and they may lack motivation to learn; furthermore, the knowledge and capability they develop will dissipate before they come to use it.

It is all too easy to fall into the trap of assuming that training and development only takes place in Phase 2. It is comforting to think "We've done the training so now everything can get back to normal". In reality, the greatest learning happens when people apply what they've learnt in earnest. This is when they realise that not everything they have learnt works as easily as it did in the classroom and there is a great temptation to revert to the old ways. Some will battle on and find their way through, but others need help and support to overcome difficulties and to keep the faith. This is where coaching, preferably by line managers, is so important in ensuring that people continue on their journey of development and that even the faint-hearted reach the destination. See Section 2.6 for details on effective training and development.

Performance management

In Chapter 6, we saw the importance of defining, communicating, measuring, recognising and rewarding success in bringing about change. Once a change has been implemented, recognition and reward for success is essential in ensuring that the change is cemented into place. The process begins with the clarification of expectations of people after the change and adjustment of their targets in line with new objectives. It is no use, for instance, expecting people to reduce error rates if they are measured and incentivised solely on productivity. But, as we saw in Chapter 6, there is a more subtle requirement on managers to encourage people who are displaying new behaviours even before they have achieved the desired results. People may be trying out new techniques for reducing errors or improving customer service but may be struggling to master them. It is quite probable that performance will fall before it improves. It may also be that the results of people's efforts will take time to filter through as measurable results. In these circumstances, it is crucial that managers recognise and encourage people who are trying out new skills and behaviours and to provide coaching and support where required.

One way to get off on the right foot is for managers to be involved in delivering training to their people ahead of the change. This not only ensures that they are seen to be clearly mandating the change it also equips them better to coach and support their teams after the change.

If leaders do not practice sound performance management the benefits of a major change may not be achieved. People may fail to adopt new methods or slip back into old ways when the new ones prove hard to master.

Lessons learned review

Once a change has been implemented there is a great opportunity to learn from successes and failures by conducting a Lessons Learned Review. This involves gathering feedback from all parties involved in or affected by the change and provides vital guidance on how to be more successful next time around. The Change Effectiveness Survey detailed in Section 9.5 is a very useful aid to this process.

9.5 Post implementation survey

Once a change has been fully installed, it is useful to elicit feedback from people about what happened so that you can improve your performance next time around. An assessment of how well you have done can be made using the Change Effectiveness Survey below. This survey should be completed by people across the organisation who have been affected by the change.

All too often, organisations get to the end of a change initiative and breathe a huge sigh of relief before running headlong at the next one. Enterprises that take stock at the end of each change initiative and are able to learn form failure and success alike will steadily increase their Organisational Adaptability to Change (see Chapter 8).

Change Effectiveness Survey

Strongly Disagree — 0 1 2 3 4 5 — Strongly Agree

Score the following statements from 0 – 5, where 0 means you "strongly disagree" and 5 means you "strongly agree".

As there are 20 questions, the maximum score for a change is 100 (extremely well implemented change) and the minimum score is zero (extremely badly implemented change).

Certainty

1. There was strong and confident leadership of change by all leaders and managers.
2. There was a clear plan for change.
3. There was extensive, open and honest communication leading up to the change.
4. Successes following the change were widely communicated.

Purpose

5. The purpose for the change has been clear throughout the change process.
6. A clear vision of the future was communicated throughout the change.
7. It is clear how the change supports the overall purpose of the organisation.
8. It is clear how the change supports the values* of the organisation.

*a common set of beliefs about how we should do things and how we should work with each other and with our customers, suppliers and the wider community.

Control

9. People affected by the change were consulted about the nature of the change and how it should happen.
10. Some of the people affected by the change were involved in formulating and implementing the change.
11. People felt well informed about the change while it was happening.
12. Different parts of the organisation had the flexibility to decide how to implement the change in their own areas.

Connection

13. The change feels like an improvement from the way things were done in the past.
14. The transition to new working practices was managed well.
15. The transition to new ways of working with other people was managed well.
16. People feel overall that they have benefited from the change.

Success

17. People have successfully mastered the new skills they require to be successful.
18. People have successfully mastered the new attitudes and behaviours to be successful.
19. People's goals and targets are aligned with new methods and objectives.
20. People are clear about what they need to do to be considered successful after the change.

Summary

Key points for leaders to note:

1. Organisational changes will succeed or fail depending on whether you harness the 5 Forces of Change in support of change or battle against them. Working with the 5 Forces of Change dispels anxieties, generates positive enthusiasm for change and creates an environment for success.

2. The 5 Forces of Change come into play in different ways during each of the three phases of change; so the focus of your effort and the tools and techniques you employ will need to vary accordingly.

Chapter 10

Change Leadership

The ability to bring about successful change is perhaps the most important skill required by a leader in a modern organisation. It is leaders, at all levels of an organisation, that must create the conditions for change to take root and ultimately to bear fruit.

Chapters 8 and 9 focused on what leaders must *do* to bring about successful change. This chapter concentrates on an effective leadership philosophy or style during times of change. In doing so, it draws together the key themes covered so far and further underlines one of the main tenets of the book that the difference between the success and failure of organisational change is leadership.

10.1 Six leadership characteristics

Great leaders work with the grain of human nature rather than against it to bring about change. Instead of battling with resistance to change, they diminish or eliminate people's motives for resisting change in the first place. This requires a certain style of leadership based on six key characteristics (see below).

To better appreciate the six characteristics of great change leadership it helps to think of a specific change that you have been involved in. Preferably, you should think of a change that took some time to implement and affected a number of people.

It may also help you to consider an example outside of work.

Imagine you are leading a group of families (100 men, women and children) on a long journey over difficult and dangerous terrain.

Between you and your destination lies thousands of miles of desolate country; dry inhospitable plains inhabited by hostile natives and treacherous mountain passes. It is over 150 years ago and you are travelling in a Wagon Train; most people are travelling in wagons pulled by horses, some are on horseback. You have to carry everything you need with you. These families are travelling in hope of a better life in a distant land they had never been to before. What might you have to do to keep everyone going through thick and thin for many weeks, perhaps months?

It is essential that you plan your journey well. You need to take on the right provisions and the right equipment. You need weapons to protect yourself from the natives and people with the ability to use them. However, you cannot anticipate all eventualities and in the end your greatest resource is the people you are travelling with. How you lead them may well be the difference between life and death.

Now consider six characteristics of great leaders of change.

1. Vision

Great change leaders have a clear vision of where they want to lead their organisation. They engage others in this vision through repeated communication and the strength of their conviction. Their desire for change is unmistakable and their enthusiasm infectious. They are not deterred from their mission by the difficulties they face along the way.

In the case of the Wagon Train journey to a new land, there will be many occasions when people doubted the wisdom of the whole enterprise. In the face of danger and privation many will want to give up and turn back. If you don't have a clear vision of why you are making the journey then you stand little chance of convincing others. It will take a passionate sense of purpose and the ability to communicate it to the whole group for you to be successful. Crucially, you will need to help people make a strong connection between the journey (and its destination) and their dreams of a better life.

Leaders with a clear sense of purpose and the ability to communicate it with passion are able to harness three of the 5 Forces of Change in particular. They are able to inspire a strong sense of *purpose* in others through their words and deeds, which in turn gives them increased feelings of *certainty* about where they are going and why they are going there. Being able to visualise the future also helps them to give up old *connections* and to connect more readily to new ways of thinking and behaving.

2. Integrity

Great change leaders have integrity. They are clear about their principles and stick to them. What they say in private matches what they say in public and is backed up by their actions.

There will be times on the Wagon Train journey when you need to make difficult decisions and stick to your principles and times when you needed to lead by example. If you do not have a clear sense of how people should work together, share resources and support one another it will be hard for you to arbitrate in the case of disputes. If you try too hard to please people at the expense of what you believe to be right then people will lose trust in you. The same is true if you ask people to do one thing whilst you do another. You need to be sure of your principles and confident in putting them into practice. This is what it means to have integrity as a leader.

Leaders with integrity are able to harness two of the 5 Forces of Change in particular. Their clarity concerning how the journey should be made and their consistency of approach breeds confidence amongst their followers and increases people level of *certainty* even as they journey into the unknown. Buying into a set of principles (or values) that guide how the journey should be made also reinforces people's sense of *purpose*.

3. Openness

Great change leaders encourage open discussion and make it acceptable for people to express feelings of discomfort about change. They don't stifle opinions or force issues underground. They are honest about not having all the answers and are keen to draw on other people's opinions whilst remaining resolute about their overall objectives.

As a leader, you need to know a lot about what is going on. If people hide the truth from you because they feel you are not interested in their opinions or because they are too scared to tell you what you might not want to hear then you are cut off from your main source of information – other people. Without knowing what people think and feel you cannot lead them, except perhaps by fear. An open leadership style, characterised by a genuine interest in what others think, is the key to ensuring that information flows freely and you are able to respond to feelings within the group.

Leaders who display openness and approachability are able to harness three of the 5 Forces of Change in particular. By promoting a free flow of information people feel well informed increasing their sense of *certainty*. Because their opinions are sought and respected they also feel more in *control*. Because they are able to express their feelings, especially their nostalgia for what they have left behind and fears about what lies ahead, they are more able to break old *connections* and to create new ones.

4. Empowerment

Great change leaders empower people at every level by involving them in the change process and ensuring that they have the right resources and skills to do the job.

The problem with dictatorship is it makes idiots of us all. If you tell people what to do and abuse them every time they step out of line they stop thinking and become dependent on you for everything. If you are taking 100 souls hundreds of miles across a barren land the last thing you need is for everything to depend on you. On the contrary, you need to tap into the vast reserves of talent you have on hand. Some people in the group will be good navigators; others will know how to care for the sick. There will be hunters, builders, entertainers, cooks, inventors and people who provide a shoulder to cry on. By giving people the opportunity to put their various talents to good use you won't need to be all things to all people. People will feel valued and fulfilled. The group will make the most of its talents and be far more successful in overcoming the obstacles that lie in its path.

Leaders who empower others are able to harness three of the 5 Forces of Change in particular. When people are involved in decision-making and encouraged to apply their talents in pursuit of a common goal they have a greater sense of *purpose* and increased feelings of **control** over how things are done as well as a sense of achievement or *success*.

5. Coaching

Great change leaders recognise people for having a go at new ways of working even when they fail. They are quick to recognise success and to support people who are struggling. They hold to account those who opt out of change and coach their fellow leaders in how to lead change successfully.

The Wagon Train journey will be fraught with setbacks. In such circumstances a leader needs to be optimistic and encouraging of others. You need to remind people regularly about how far they have come and the many difficulties they have overcome. You need to keep people's spirits up by thanking those who have, for instance, helped others in some way or done more than their fair share of work.

Leaders who coach and support others are able to harness two of the 5 Forces of Change in particular. When people are listened to, encouraged and supported they get a clearer idea of they need to do to succeed and feel more **successful** when they achieve their goals. People who are coached also have a greater sense of **certainty** that they are heading in the right direction.

6. Consensus

Great change leaders build consensus for change amongst their fellow leaders and work with them to tip the balance of opinion in favour of change within the wider population.

In the middle of a battle with hoards of hostile natives would not the time to take a vote on what to do next. It would be a time for decisive action. But such times would be few and far between (at least you would hope so if you going to survive they journey). In quieter times, you will need a high degree of consensus amongst your group of hopeful travellers. By listening to people and observing how they behave you will quickly learn which people hold sway with others, who communicates the most and who is respected by others. You will sort the optimists from the pessimists, the leaders from the followers, and the carers from the thinkers. To lead the group you will need to know what's going on by talking to the networkers (people that everyone else talks to) and to build consensus with the people others look to for leadership. You need the optimists to help encourage others and give energy to the group and you may chose to keep some sceptics close to you to stop them from spreading negative feelings. Without this effort you run the risk of the group becoming divided and wasting precious energy on internal faction fighting rather than focusing it on the job in hand.

Leaders who seek consensus are able to harness two of the 5 Forces of Change in particular. When people feel that their opinions are being listened to and taken into account they will more in **control** of their destiny and are far more likely to buy into the decisions made by leaders. Where consensus and cooperation is actively promoted people will also feel a strong sense of common **purpose** and will be more willing to go the extra mile for the group.

By adopting these six leadership characteristics you will build certainty, help people maintain a sense of purpose and a sense of control, help them break old connections and forge new ones, and to persevere and succeed despite the difficulties they encounter. In this way, you will engage people's hearts and minds in driving change forward.

If the prospect of taking on all the traits of a great change leader puts you off the idea of taking charge of change then think of them more as an ideal and as a target to aim for. Also, where you perceive you have a weakness you can call on others in your team to support you. You may, for instance, have people in your team who love connecting to lots of other people and are able to build wide-ranging consensus for change where perhaps you are less able.

Something else to consider is how you can apply the 5 Forces of Change to yourself to further develop your leadership capability.

10.2 Leading yourself through change

As we saw above, success in leading others through change is dependent on your own behaviour. So unless you can manage and direct this behaviour it will be impossible for you to lead others well. You can use The 5 Forces of Change to lead yourself both in your personal and professional life as well as in leading other people.

Consider two examples of change, one personal and one professional. Imagine, for instance, that you are unfit and want to get fitter and as a leader you want to become more empowering of others. How might you apply the 5 Forces of Change to yourself? Table 10.1 lists some possible actions you might take to ensure that you are successful in achieving these two goals. As can be seen from the table, you can use the 5 Forces of Change as a framework for leading yourself more effectively to your chosen goals as well as in leading others through change.

	Get Fit	Become a More Empowering Leader
Certainty	• Read advice from professionals on the best methods of getting fit • Find out about people who have succeeded in getting fit and how they did it • Identify why you have failed to get fit before and find ways to overcome these obstacles • Set a clear target • Create a fitness plan specifying your fitness routine and milestones • Keep a fitness record to gain confidence from what you have achieved	• Find out what empowering others really involves • Identify why you have not empowered people before and find ways to overcome these obstacles • Take advice from people who are very empowering of others • Set out an action plan for empowering the people that work with you • Get feedback from people on how they think you are doing against your goal
Purpose	• Identify a really important personal reason why you want to get fit (how will being fit help you achieve other things that are very important to you?) • Set a challenging and clear target e.g. to run a half marathon • Visualise future success (How will you look and feel?)	• Understand why you want to empower people (how will it help you achieve other goals that are important to you?) • Set a challenging a clear targets • Visualise what it would be like to have an empowered team (How would things look and feel?)
Control	• Do it for yourself not to please others • Become informed about the best ways to get fit • Set your own goals and your own fitness plan • Record your progress	• Do it because you believe in it not because others say you should • Become informed about the best ways to empower others • Set your own goals and your own action plan • Record your progress and get feedback from other people

	Get Fit	**Become a More Empowering Leader**
Connection	• Work out what you lose by becoming fit e.g. time do other things or fitting in with other unfit people • Make a ceremonial break with the past e.g. burn a list of past excuses for not getting fit • Declare your goals to others • Get a 'fitness buddy' – someone who will get fit alongside you; someone to rely on for support and encouragement, and who relies on you for the same	• Work out what you lose by empowering other e.g. feeling in control of things • Make a ceremonial break with the past e.g. eliminate a symbol of control such as an overly detailed progress report • Declare your goals to others • Share your goals with a 'buddy' – a colleague who also want to develop their leadership capabilities; someone to rely on for support and feedback and who relies on you for the same
Success	• Define your overall goal clearly (I will be fit when…) • Get coaching from a 'fitness buddy' (see above) • Set short term as well as long term goals • Measure progress towards your goals • Celebrate mini successes	• Define what success looks like (I will be an empowering leader when…) • Get coaching from your 'buddy' (see above) • Set short term as well as long term goals • Measure progress towards your goals • Celebrate mini successes

Figure 10.1 Actions you might take to get fit and to become a more empowering leader

Summary

1. To harness the 5 Forces of Change effectively requires a leadership style characterised by vision, integrity, openness, empowerment, coaching and consensus

2. You can harness the 5 Forces of Change to improve your own performance as well as in leading others through change.

References

Chapter 1

1. Beer, M. and Nohria, N. (2000) Cracking the code of change, Harvard Business Review, May/June, 133-141.
2. Hammer, M., Champy, J. (1993), Reengineering the Corporation, Harper Business, New York, NY (1999).
3. Mergers and Acquisitions: Global Research Report (1999). London: KPMG.
4. Motivation and Personality, 3rd Edition, Abraham Maslow
5. Herzberg on Motivation (1983), Frederick Herzberg.

Chapter 2

1. www.prosci.com
2. Managing at the Speed of Change, Daryl R Conner, Vaillard Books

Chapter 3

1. Built to Last, 3rd Edition, James C. Collins & Jerry I. Porras, Random House (2000)
2. Managing at the Speed of Change, Daryl R Conner, Vaillard Books

Chapter 4

1. www.bestcompanies.co.uk
2. Work, Stress, Health – the Whitehall Study II, Published by Public and Commercial Services Union on behalf of Council of Civil Service Unions/Cabinet Office (2004)
3. Rawmarsh School, Rotherham, September 2006, photograph Ross Parry Agency
4. Source of data: Bosma, H., Peter R., Seigrist J., and Marmot M.G. (1998)
5. Tannenbaum, R. and Schmidt, W. (1958) How to choose a leadership pattern, Harvard Business Review 36(2), 95-101

Chapter 5

1. Timeline Therapy and the Basis of Personality, Tad James & Wyatt Woodsnall, Meta Publications (1988)
2. Gifts Differing: Understanding Personality Type (Paperback) by Isabel Briggs Myers and Peter B. Myers, Davies-Black Publishing (1995)

Chapter 7

1. Diffusion of Innovations, Fifth Edition, Everett M. Rogers New York, NY: Free Press (2003)
2. Weight Loss With Self-help Compared With a Structured Commercial Program, Journal of the American Medical Association, Vol. 289 No. 14, April 9, 2003

Index